The Political History of Eastern Europe in the 20th Century

The Political History of Eastern Europe in the 20th Century

The Struggle Between Democracy and Dictatorship

By
Sten Berglund
University of Örebro, Sweden
and
Frank Aarebrot
University of Bergen, Norway

Edward Elgar
Cheltenham, UK • Lyme, US

Published by
Edward Elgar Publishing Limited
8 Lansdown Place
Cheltenham
Glos GL50 2HU
UK

Edward Elgar Publishing, Inc.
1 Pinnacle Hill Road
Lyme
NH 03768
US

A catalogue record for this book is available from the British Library

Library of Congress Cataloguing-in-Publication Data

Berglund, Sten, 1947–
    The political history of Eastern Europe in the 20th century : the stuggle between democracy and dictatorship / by Sten Berglund and Frank H. Aarebot.
    Includes bibliographical references and indexes.
    1. Europe, Eastern—Politics and government—20th century.
2. Authoritarianism—Europe, Eastern. 3. Communism—Europe, Eastern. 4. Democracy—Europe, Eastern. I. Aarebrot, Frank H., 1947– . II. Title. III. Series.
DJK49.B473 1997   96–41938
947.084—dc20
                                                                    CIP

ISBN 1 85898 478 5

Printed and bound in Great Britain by Hartnolls Limited, Bodmin, Cornwall

Contents

Tables and Figures

Tables

Figures

Notes on the Authors

Sten Berglund (born 1947), is professor of political science at the universities of Uppsala and Örebro in Sweden. He has published a number of articles and books on parties and party systems, including *The Scandinavian Party Systems* (Lund, Studentlitteratur, 1978) and *Paradoxes of Political Parties* (Umeå, Liber, 1980). He has co-authored a volume on *Democracy and Foreign Policy* (Longmead, Gower, 1986) and co-edited and co-authored a volume on *The New Democracies in Eastern Europe: Party Systems and Political Cleavages* (Aldershot, Edward Elgar, 1991; 1994).

Frank Aarebrot (born 1947) is associate professor in political science at the University of Bergen in Norway. He is the author and co-author of numerous articles and chapters within the field of comparative politics, among others: 'On the Structural Basis of Regional Variation in Europe' in De Marcchi & Boileau *Boundaries and Minorities in Western Europe* (Milan, Franco Angeli, 1982), 'The Politics of Cultural Dissent: Religion Language and Demonstrative Effects in Norway' with Derek Urwin, in *Scandivaian Political Studies* 1979:2 and 'Analysis and Explanation of Variation in Territorial Structure' in Stein Rokkan et al. *Centre-Periphery Structures in Europe* (Frankfurt a.M, Campus, 1987).

Sten Berglund and Frank Aarebrot have previously co-authored several articles on European comparative politics including two chapters on Eastern Europe and the EFTA countries in Oscar Niedermayer and Richard Sinnott, eds: *Public Opinion and Internationalized Governance* (Oxford, Oxford University Press, 1995).

Preface

This book on *The Political History of Eastern Europe in the 20th Century: The Struggle between Democracy and Dictatorship* is a product of the authors' long-standing interest in political transition. The focus is not only on the dramatic events of 1989–90 and the subsequent return to political pluralism in Eastern Europe. The book addresses itself to the three democratic options that history has dealt Eastern Europe during this century: the inter-war era (1917–39), the democratic or semi-democratic interlude in the wake of the Second World War (1945–49) as well as the current experiment in democracy. A great deal of attention is also devoted to the question of diversity and pluralism during the drawn-out communist parenthesis of 1949–89.

The approach is based on comparative political science and macro-sociology. This kind of comparative approach with its emphasis on conceptual schemes always leads to a certain loss of information, but this is a price well worth paying in view of the theory-building potential. We believe that this volume on the struggle between democracy and dictatorship has something to say about the conditions for democratic survival and breakdown particularly in Eastern Europe. We are confident that the book provides a number of useful analytical distinctions and structuring criteria for political scientists with an interest in regime change.

*

We are indebted to a number of institutions and colleagues whose support and assistance have been of vital importance. The book was written while Sten Berglund was affiliated with professor Hans-Dieter Klingemann's research unit at the Science Center (WZB) in Berlin within the framework of a research award from the Alexander von Humboldt Foundation in Bonn. Sten Berglund wishes to avail himself of this opportunity to thank the Alexander von Humboldt Foundation for its generosity and professor Klingemann and his associates for providing him with one of the best environments there is for research on Eastern Europe. Frank Aarebrot wishes to thank colleagues at the Department for Comparative Politics at the University of Bergen, particularly professor Stein Kuhnle and associate professor Einar Berntzen, for their encouragement and support.

We are also indebted to professor Russel Dalton of the University of California at Irvine, who made the Times–Mirror data base available to us; to the Science Center (WZB) which gave us access to the impressive data bank on social and political indicators compiled by Charles Taylor and his associates and to the Norwegian Social Science Data Service (NSD) in Bergen which provided us with one Eurobarometer study after another. We alone bear responsibility for the analyses and interpretations, but there would have been preciously little by way of empirical analyses if it had not been for the willingness of these scholars and institutions to share relevant East European data with us.

We are also indebted to Dr Tomas Hellén, Mr Christian Lindblom, and Mr Henri Vogt, all of Helsinki, for providing valuable input along the way and particularly towards the end of a long research process. Last but by no means least, we would like to mention the unconditional support and encouragement of our respective wives – Mrs Ulla Berglund and Marianne Flick – and children, who accepted a tight time table almost without complaint.

Sten Berglund   Frank Aarebrot
Berlin   Bergen

1. The Heritage

The Beginning of the End

With the benefit of hindsight, the last few decades prior to the First World War (1914–18) spelled the beginning of the end for the Austro-Hungarian, German, Russian and Ottoman empires, some of which had dominated Central and East European politics for centuries. In figure 1.1 we have superimposed the imperial spheres of influence on the current map of Europe. As will become apparent throughout this book, the impact of the empires makes itself felt even today (Klingemann 1994).

Figure 1.1 The former imperial spheres of influence and the present borders

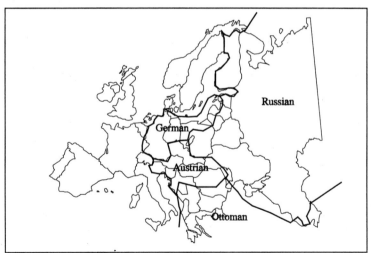

The most recent arrival in the imperial sphere – the German *Kaiserreich* (1870–1918) – had the best odds for survival. It was an empire, but with a solid Prussian state core and thus far removed from Eisenstadt's concept of historical empires, where statehood is relegated to a subordinate position (Eisenstadt 1963). In theory the Austro-Hungarian empire (1526–1918) had an Austrian state core, but for all intents and purposes the Habsburg dual monarchy also had a Hungarian state core (Kann 1977a). Vienna somehow had to come to terms with Budapest; and as if this were not enough, the authority of the empire was constantly challenged by a variety of subordinate nationalities, most notably by the Czechs and the Yugoslavs. Looking back on the dissolution of the Habsburg empire and the survival of Germany in the form of the Weimar republic in 1918, Rudolf Kjellén draws the following conclusion:

> A Great Power can endure without difficulty one Ireland, as England did, even three, as imperial Germany did (Poland, Alsace, Schleswig). Different is the case when a Great Power is composed of nothing else but Irelands, as was almost the history of Austro–Hungary .... (Kjellén 1921).

Similar comments apply to the Ottoman (1453–1918) and Russian (1492–1917) historical empires. By the beginning of the 20th century, the feudal Ottoman empire was a great power in decline. It had lost the lion's share of its substantial possessions on the Balkan peninsula – including Bulgaria and Romania which gained formal independence in 1878 – to the rivalling Russian and Austro–Hungarian empires as a result of popular uprisings sponsored by the neighbouring great powers throughout the 19th century (Tilly 1993). After its humiliating defeat by Japan in 1904, Russia was also in a sense a great power in retreat. The domestic repercussions of the military *débâcle* had put Russia on the road towards constitutional rule, but, though important as such, the reforms were not sufficient to put an end to the turmoil and ethnic tensions that had plagued the Russian empire for decades.

By the beginning of the century, pressure for change was running high all over Central and Eastern Europe. In Germany, which had come out of the 19th century as a leading industrial and military power, the parties of the left, most notably the Social Democratic Party, kept pushing for democracy and parliamentarism. In Austria-Hungary, the emphasis was on national autonomy and even national independence for the various national groups united by their historically conditioned ties to the Habsburg Crown. The struggle for democracy became equated with the struggle for national independence and vice versa just as it had been in Italy and to some extent in Germany prior to unification in 1870. But there were also serious attempts to defuse the nationality issue of its potentially explosive character by disentangling it from the territorial dimensions. To that end, the socialist deputy Karl Renner (1870–1950), subsequently chancellor of the first and second Austrian republics, introduced a scheme, which left it to the individual citizens of multi-ethnic areas to determine their national affiliation. They were then eligible to vote in national *curiae*, German, Czech or whatever, for a predetermined number of deputies. Some public matters, particularly the controversial cultural and educational matters, were to be administered by nationally homogeneous agencies. In 1905 a compromise of this kind was reached between Germans and Czechs in Moravia; another in 1910 between Ruthenians, Romanians, Germans and Jews in the Bukovina, and the enactment of a third in Galicia between Poles and Ruthenians was only blocked by the outbreak of the First World War (Kann 1980, 442).

The German and Austro-Hungarian empires had recently embarked on the road towards constitutional monarchy. Though broad and vague, there were definite limits to the realm of competence of the two emperors; there were formal and legal ways of reforming the system and as of the early 1870s and the early 1900s, there was universal suffrage to parliamentary assemblies not entirely without influence in Germany and in Austria respectively (Craig 1983; 1995). Unlike the Russian and Ottoman empires, the German and Austro-Hungarian empires provided a setting, which was not favourable to reform, but definitely did not rule it out.

Lenin was not far off the mark, when referring to the revolutionary role of the communist party – then known as the social democratic party – in the clandestine struggle against the 'darkness of the autocracy' (Lenin 1905; 1963). The constitutional reforms in the wake of the defeat in the Russo–Japanese War were never fully implemented; the role of the *Duma* – which was boycotted by the radical left – was unilaterally curtailed by the Tsar (Tilly 1993) and Lenin and his followers remained prime targets of the *Ochrana*, the imperial secret police, until the October revolution of 1917. The Ottoman empire – the other outlier in the European context – was open to economic and military modernization, but remained even further removed than Russia from the mainstream European political thought on nationalism, democracy and parliamentarism.

The writing may have been on the wall, but to the extent that it was, few, if any, were able to decipher it.[1] At the turn of the century, the German, Austro-Hungarian and perhaps even the Russian empires seemed to have had long term prospects for survival as political entities. There was unprecedented economic progress; Berlin, Vienna and St Petersburg remained flourishing cultural centres throughout the late 1800s and early 1900s; there was a potential for gradual and piecemeal change; and last but not least, the existing order was not questioned until the very last stage of the First World War – the *ancien régime* did indeed work admirably until the bitter end (Crankshaw 1963, 1994). The fate of the Russian empire was sealed by the Russian revolution of October 1917, by the subsequent separate peace treaty with Germany in Brest–Litovsk in February 1918 and by the appropriation by the Bolsheviks of the cause of the oppressed national minorities. The fate of the Habsburg empire was sealed by its failure to comply with a Franco-British request for a separate peace agreement at the expense of Germany, but until late 1917, perhaps even early 1918, Georges Clémenceau and Lloyd George, the French and British prime ministers, nevertheless counted on preserving the Austro-Hungarian monarchy as a political entity (Johnson 1994, 20–21). The failure to preserve the Austro–Hungarian monarchy in some form or other and the failure of the subsequent peace treaties 1919 in Versailles, Neuilly and Trianon to provide for lasting peace have frequently been blamed on the naivety of Woodrow Wilson, the only political scientist so far to become president of the United States, and on his insistence on national self-determination. Johnson (1994) has a point, when suggesting that Wilson's hands were forced by the duplicity of his British and French allies, who had refrained from informing the United States about a variety of outstanding commitments to potential partners in the war against Germany, and by the timely and expedient pledge by the Bolsheviks to the cause of national self-determination.

But this is a matter for further historical research. Applying an empirical rather than an idealistic perspective, we conclude that the First World War resulted in the destruction of the imperial structure in Europe. The successors states – including Estonia, Latvia, Lithuania, Poland, Czechoslovakia and Yugoslavia – were numerous and often without strong historical credentials.[2] But whether devolved from the core of the defunct empires or from the periphery of these empires, the new states were largely conditioned by their imperial past.

We have already dwelled at some length on one aspect of relevance in this context – the relationship between nationalism and democracy. We have suggested that the territorial solutions imposed by the Western allies in Versailles, Neuilly and Trianon did not lack conflict potential. And we have at least touched upon another aspect of equal importance – the impact of modernization with all which that entailed by way of industrialization, urbanization and secularization.

The Challenge of Nationalism

Nationalism is a multi-faceted phenomenon and there are almost as many definitions of the concept on the market as there are scholars with an interest in it. Of particular interest to us is the relationship between state and nation. Do nationalistic aspirations go beyond the current state boundaries or do they coincide with them? Do they threaten or support existing state structures? And, last but not least, are the nationalistic aspirations cast in aggressive terms or are they not?

Nationalism always has an element of exclusion to it. As Deutsch (1963) put it, nationalism gives preferential treatment to messages with the right source symbols attached to them. But nationalism can be more or less exclusive. The most extreme kind of nationalism would ignore, reject or at least belittle messages which come with the wrong source tag on them. The least exclusive and most moderate kind of nationalism would only be inclined to give a minimum of preferential treatment to messages from the 'right' sources.

There are at least two kinds of states. There are homogeneous nation-states and heterogeneous multi-ethnic states. The former are dominated by one nationality which is swayed by more or less exclusive national sentiments either to the benefit or to the detriment of the status quo. The latter may be dominated by one single nationality, but – to the extent that the dominant nationality does not opt for all-out repression – it will somehow have to come to terms with the national aspirations of the competing nationalities. In this particular setting, even moderate expressions of nationalism may be detrimental to the survival of the regime as well as to international stability, at least to the extent that they do not embrace the notion of a multi-ethnic nation as in the case of Switzerland.

*

The German *Reich* that emerged in 1870 was definitely a nation-state. Situated in the middle of Europe and sharing borders with six other countries, Imperial Germany was not entirely without minority problems, though. There were more than scattered groups of Alsatians, Danes and Poles, but they did not account for much in terms of sheer numbers (Immerfall 1992, 151–7). On the other hand, there were sizable German settlements outside the borders of the *Kaiserreich*, particularly in Austria, Bohemia and Moravia. This was not perceived as a problem by Bismarck, the principal architect of German unity, who was fearful of disrupting the delicate balance of power in Europe. In fact German diaspora did not become a serious problem until the National Socialists embarked on a campaign designed to incorporate all Germans, including the Austrians and the *Sudeten* Germans, into one *Reich*. Similar comments apply to anti-Semitism which played a minor role in Imperial Germany and developed into the very essence of the National Socialism of the Third *Reich*.

Tapping the intellectual climate – the *Zeitgeist* as it were – even of a rather recent past is an awesome task fraught with pitfalls. But on the basis of available evidence, we would nevertheless venture to draw the conclusion that German nationalism was a rather mainstream Central and West European phenomenon prior to the First World War. It was self-glorifying, but nationalism generally is. It was chauvinistic and imperialistic, but this was an era of unprecedented competition for colonies among the great powers. It is true that German nationalism had a strongly pronounced authoritarian streak to it. It is also true that it was heavily influenced by an almost metaphysical understanding of key concepts in the contemporary political discourse like people, nation and state and that it was inclined to adopt a Darwinistic approach towards the competition for power among nations. But in this respect, German nationalism was rather similar to French nationalism. To the extent that there was a watershed in European conservative political thought prior to the First World War, it ran between the *absolute* conservatism of Continental Europe and the *pragmatic* Burkean kind of conservatism prevalent in the United Kingdom. Though advocates of conflicting national causes, Germany's Heinrich von Treitschke and Maurice Barrès and Charles Maurras of France were all exponents and apostles of what Craig (1995, 197) refers to as 'totalitarian nationalism'. Germany – and France for that matter – thus provided fertile soil for the extreme kind of nationalism, but the extreme nationalism long coexisted with the moderate variety and did not gain the upper hand until the war, which it had help bring about, had become reality.

*

The Austro-Hungarian monarchy was a multi-ethnic empire from the very beginning. But it was a multi-ethnic empire with a state core in the Austrian hereditary lands of the Habsburg monarchy which provided the platform for the subsequent acquisition of the Eastern crowns of Hungary, Croatia and Bohemia. The emperor was German; the centralized bureaucracy – on which the emperor was dependent in order to keep abreast of events and developments within his huge realm – built the vast empire in German; and, to all intents and purposes, there was hardly any cultural life in languages other than German and possibly Latin.[3]

There were several attempts to Germanize the non-German parts of the empire, including the famous language decree of 1784 by Joseph II which proclaimed German as the only language of instruction in the empire (Kann 1980, 192–208). The decree met with such resistance that it had to be revoked a few years later. And, on the whole, the Austro-Germans had stopped proselytizing by the time they were confronted with the call for autonomy, self-determination and even total independence from all four corners of the empire in the middle of the 19th century.

In theory the imperial government had the classical choice between reform and repression. It opted for a little of both; but – with the benefit of hindsight – we know that it was too little and too late. The political reforms stopped considerably short of the federal solution which might have solved the minority problems once and for all as is sometimes argued (Jászi 1929; Kann 1977a, 1977b, 1980). The government went for compromise, but only with Hungary which was promoted to a position of formal equality with Austria in most respects, but by no means in all, by virtue of the formal treaty between Austria and Hungary known as the Compromise of 1867. Though vague and open to a variety of interpretations, the Compromise removed the Hungarian issue from the agenda, but it did not do much to improve the lot of the other nationalities within the vast empire. The Compromise was in fact bad news particularly for the Croats, the

Romanians and Serbs within the Hungarian sphere of interest who found themselves subjected to a harsh and unchecked policy of Magyarization, but it was also received with dismay by the Czechs who had been entertaining high hopes for a constitutional arrangement settling their national grievances with Austria.

The dualism of the Austro-Hungarian Compromise did not put an end to the ethnic diversity of the Habsburg empire. The vast majority of the many ethnic groups had well defined geopolitical strongholds, where they enjoyed a certain political and cultural autonomy. They remained relevant political actors until the formal demise of the empire in 1918; and in their attempts to preserve the status quo the rulers of Austria and Hungary were always ready to strike a deal in order to secure the support and loyalty of one ethnic group in the struggle against another. Hungary worked out a separate compromise with Croatia as early as 1868; and during the last few years of the empire there were even serious attempts by Renner, Jászi and others to work out what might have been a permanent solution to the ethnic problems of the empire by depoliticizing the territorial dimension of the nationality problem.

It was military defeat in the First World War that sealed the fate of the Austro-Hungarian empire. It is a moot question what would have happened to the empire, if the world war had not intervened. As already mentioned, the Austro-Hungarian monarchy was an ethnically highly fragmented society and as such sensitive even to moderate expressions of nationalism, to say nothing of the extreme and highly exclusive kind of nationalism which flared up from time to time in the form of pan-German, pan-Slav or Yugoslav movements.[4] And as if this were not enough, the constitutional foundations of the empire were archaic and extremely poorly equipped for integrating the strong centrifugal forces unleashed by struggle for national autonomy by the various national groups within the empire. In this sense, the odds were heavily tilted against system survival from the very beginning of the national revolution in Europe, even though there was indeed evidence of an all-embracing Austro-Hungarian identity until the final days of the First World War.

*

In a historical perspective, the Russians had been empire builders rather than state builders, and as such the Tsars had always been open to a variety of administrative solutions in the various fiefdoms of the vast empire provided that taxes were paid and recruits supplied (Tilly 1993). The Russian speakers of Russia, Belorussia and the Ukraine enjoyed a privileged position in what was basically a multi-ethnic empire under the sway of a pan-Slav movement. The Russian empire was not unaffected by the call for national independence from imperial structures that swept over Europe from the middle of the 19th century and onwards, but the impact thereof was somewhat mitigated by the fact that the vast majority of the nationalities in this huge empire were what is sometimes referred to as 'nationalities without history', i.e. nationalities without previous experience of national independence. But there had been more than scattered manifestations of national unrest in the European parts of the empire – Poland, Finland, Estonia, Latvia and Lithuania – ever since the 1860s. It is hardly coincidental that these countries were to break out of the empire in the wake of the Russian revolution of 1917.

Of all the problems confronting the archaic imperial structure in Russia, the rampant social inequality was the most serious one. Serfdom had been abolished in 1861, but this did not put an end to the pauperization of the countryside. In fact, it may even be argued that the abolition of serfdom made things worse for the peasantry. The abolition had been accompanied by a land reform which gave the peasants an opportunity to buy one half of the land which they had tilled but as communal and *not* as individual property. The landed gentry, therefore, remained a powerful economic force in the country-side even after the land reform; and the abolition of feudalism set it free to exploit the peasants on a purely market basis. On top of this, there was the impact of rapid industrialization, rapid population growth and rapid urbanization. The net result was an unprecedented wave of social unrest.

In 1899–1901 there were constant confrontations between state authorities and students at the universities of St Petersburg and Kiev which culminated in the assassination of the Minister of Education. In 1902 there was a large-scale peasant rebellion involving peasants from 175 Ukrainian villages. The following year there was a massive strike wave in southern Russia and the number of political trials kept increasing from one year to another. There was ample evidence that the Tsarist regime was rejected by intellectuals, workers and peasants alike (Tilly 1993, 310). The revolutions of 1905 and 1917 should not have come as a surprise to the *Ochrana*.

*

If there ever was a historical empire in Eisenstadt's sense (1963), it was the Ottoman empire. The rulers of this empire were even more open to feudal power sharing arrangements than the Russian Tsars as evidenced by the Turkish reaction to the recurring uprisings in its European provinces and the increasing military pressure from the European foreign powers throughout the 19th century. Faced with this dual challenge, the Ottoman empire sought to retain control of the Balkans through a set of very pragmatic and area specific compromises, from the continuation of the satrap system in Serbia to the recognition of the Bulgarian Tsar as a vassal and the peculiar system of Greek and Turkish power sharing in Romania, the so-called phanariot system (Microsoft Encarta).

Figure 1.2 Empires classified by stateness and ethnic homogeneity

Ethnic composition	Empire states	Historical empires
Homogeneous	Germany	Russia
	Austria Hungary	
Heterogeneous		The Ottoman empire

Russia also qualifies as a historical empire (see figure 1.2). The external challengers were there as evidenced by the Crimean War (1853–5) and the Russo–Japanese War (1904–5), but the impact of these challenges was less severe than in the Ottoman empire which found itself in an all but constant state of siege from the Greek rebellion of 1829 and onwards. Imperial Russia was ethnically more homogeneous and had a stronger core population than the Ottoman empire, but both empires had preciously little by way of state building traditions and pledged allegiance to a basically feudal form of government.

Of the three empire states, Imperial Germany was ethnically homogeneous enough to qualify as a nation-state. The two protagonists of the Austro-Hungarian dual monarchy fell considerably shorter in this dimension, but, crude as our rough estimates may be, it is nevertheless worth noting that the Austrian and Hungarian empire states had state cores backed up by sizeable German and Magyar core populations.

At the turn of the century, there were thus three alternative national concepts on the European political market. There was the German *Volkstaat* or nation-state model; there was the Austrian *Staatsvolk* model with a strong core population dominating a state including subject minorities; and there were the Hungarian-style national empires with a small ethnically defined core population dominating substantial ethnic minorities.

The Territorial Challenge

Two factors have to be taken into account, when evaluating the various nationalist movements of Eastern and Central Europe at the turn of the century with respect to their ability to challenge the territorial integrity of their respective empires. The demands made by the nationalist movements could be more or less severe and cover the full range from cultural autonomy to full fledged independence with federal solutions as an intermediate position.

The varying severity of the territorial challenge is of interest in its own right, but we are also concerned with the propensity of the imperial regimes to view the various levels of autonomy demanded by the nationalist groups as a threat to the territorial integrity of the empire. In some cases, even mild demands would be perceived as serious threats and in other cases even far reaching demands might be met with attempts at compromise by the central authorities. The former were characterized by a low level of tolerance and the latter by a high level of tolerance.

Once again the type of empire turns out to be of decisive importance. The alternative state formations challenging the empire states must at all times consider the reactions of the national core populations which reduces their room of manoeuvre. In this setting, potential nationalist movements will have to make extreme or separatist

Figure 1.3 A framework for understanding nationalist movements within the empires

The national concept \ The territorial challenge	Alternative state formation (Devolved from empire states)	Interface territories defined by conflicting imperial aspirations (Devolved from historical empires)
Homogeneous population: The *Volkstaat* model	Thomas Masaryk's original vision of a Bohemian–Moravian republic	Estonian, Latvian and Lithuanian nationalism
	Prussia–Germany	Moldavia and Vallachia
		Montenegro
	Polish nationalists in Germany and Austria	Congress Poland
Strong core population, but including subject minorities: The *Staatsvolk* model	The Austrian part of the dual monarchy	Tsarist visions of a pan-slavic empire
		Original concept of a Serbian homeland
		Bulgaria
Ethnically based new national empires: Substantial subject populations	Magyarism: Greater Hungary	Romania's Transylvanian aspirations
		Greater Serbia and the Southern Slav Movement (Yugoslavia)
		Greater Albania
		An extreme example: Turkish nationalists dreaming of an empire of Turkish–speaking peoples from the Bosporus to Sinkiang

demands in order to prevail over the central authorities. The potential territorial challengers of the historical empires find themselves in an entirely different situation. The historical empires have a high tolerance of diversity and are inclined towards feudal-style compromises with aspiring nationalities; and unlike the nationalist movements of the empire states, their counterparts in the historical empires often occupy what may be referred to as interface territories at the intersection of two imperial spheres of interest. This adds a foreign-policy dimension to the struggle for autonomy within the historical empires which is often part and parcel of the struggle between two empires. It may in fact be argued that the nationalist movements of the historical empires sought to substitute one feudal lord for another rather than fight for independence. In this particular setting the nationalist struggle more often than not centred on the relative advantages and disadvantages of the two rivalling feudal lords (see figure 1.3).

Rough as our categories might be, it is, nevertheless, instructive to compare the various exponents of the three national concepts in their respective historical settings. Thomas Masaryk's original concept of a Bohemian–Moravian republic, Bismarck's concept of a German nation-state with a Prussian core and the concept of a Polish nation-state advocated by the Polish parties of the German *Reichstag* and the Austrian *Reichsrat* are theoretically no different than the *Volkstaat* models embraced by Estonian, Latvian and Lithuanian nationalists. Similar comments apply to the Romanian proponents of the principalities of Moldavia and Vallachia, to the notion of a Montenegrian kingdom and, of course, to the independence movement in Congress Poland, i.e. the part of Poland under Russian administration since the Congress of Vienna in 1815. But there is at least one fundamental difference between Czech, German and the Western brand of Polish nationalism, on the one hand, and the ethnically defined nationalist movements of the Russian and Turkish periphery, on the other: the strongly pronounced foreign policy dimension in the historical empires. The recurring rebellions in Congress Poland always resulted in tensions between Russia, on the one hand, and Austria and Prussia–Germany, on the other. The Baltic nationalists looked to Germany for support. The Romanian nationalists of Moldavia and Valachia played the complicated game of seeking autonomy within the Ottoman empire, while rallying support for independence from abroad; and the Montenegrian nationalists played the Byzantine game of Balkan power politics with no less skill.

The impact of the foreign policy dimension becomes even more readily apparent as we move to the proponents of what we have referred to as the *Staatsvolk* model as well as to the new national empires. The vast majority of the cases on the right hand side (see figure 1.3) pertain to the Balkans, the very epitome of an interface territory. But it is also worth noting that Austria and Hungary stand out as the only representatives of the last two national concepts. The first model – the *Staatsvolk* model – is particularly suitable in a distinctly feudal environment. Austria did have feudal traits, but as time went by they became less pronounced and by the turn of the century they were certainly less distinct than the feudal traditions of Russia and Turkey. The second model – the new national empires – is also suitable in a feudal environment, but not in any feudal environment. The ruling ethnic group must not only be committed to feudal practices. It must also be able and willing to suppress the national aspirations of the substantial subject populations under its jurisdiction. The Hungarian policy of Magyarization throughout the Hungarian crownlands in the aftermath of the Austro-Hungarian Compromise of 1867 was basically repressive; the welfare of the subjugated peoples was certainly of minor importance to the advocates of Greater Romania – including predominantly Hungarian Transylvania, to the advocates of Greater Serbia – including predominantly Albanian Kosovo, and to the advocates of Greater Albania – including large parts of Greece.

In other words, as we move from North to South in our diagram, it becomes abundantly clear that the territorial solutions advocated by the nationalist movements were not likely to result in ethnically homogene-ous havens. On the contrary, it would be reasonable to argue that an increase in the number of states along the lines suggested by the various nationalist groups would have had an even greater potential for ethnic tensions and conflicts than the *ancien régime*.

But diversity in Central and Eastern Europe was not only a byproduct of nationalism. Parallel to the increasing nationalist ferment, new social divides made themselves felt.

The Challenge of Messianism

The rapid social transformation of Russia and Eastern Europe in the latter part of the 19th century and early part of the 20th century provided fertile ground for a variety of political movements which cast themselves as the panacea for all social evils from poverty to injustice. They were Messianic movements in the sense that they emphasized distant utopia rather than engaging in day-to-day politics and practical reform on the assumption that an ideal state of affairs – and only an ideal state of affairs – would remedy all evils. In retrospect, the Russian brand of Marxism as interpreted by Lenin stands out as the most important of these Messianic movements. It was to have a lasting impact on Russian and European politics for well over three quarters of a century; and Eastern Europe and Russia are still struggling to overcome this deeply rooted Marxist–Leninist ideological heritage.

Lenin's followers did not perceive the communist movement as a Messsianic movement. Marx had after all dissociated himself from Proudhon and other so-called utopian socialists and based his call for revolution on what he believed were hard scientific facts.[5] But the fact remains that the goal which Marx held out – an abundant classless society which complied with the principle 'from each according to ability and to each according to need' without the overtowering presence of a repressive state – was no less utopian than the ideals of other utopian socialists. Marx perceived the industrial proletariat as the revolutionary force *par excellence* and expected the supposedly inevitable revolutionary change to be initiated by leading European industrial nations like Great Britain, France and Germany. And there were indeed aborted attempts by local communists to stage a revolution in Austria, Hungary and Germany, but only after and *not* before the Russian revolution of October 1917 (Craig 1995, 419–21).

Theoretically, the Russian revolution revolved around the industrial proletariat. But, though reeling under the impact of rapid industrialization with all which that entailed by way of pauperization and social disintegration, Russia had remained basically rural; and the self-appointed guardians of the working class within Lenin's Bolshevik party clearly would not have succeeded in their bid for power had they not been able to enlist the support of 'the toiling masses' in general in what turned into a bloody civil war between whites and reds and between Mensheviks and Bolsheviks.[6] The campaign against the landed gentry and in favour of land reform to the advantage of the landless peasants represented a major deviation from the general commitment to collective as opposed to individual solutions to the economic plight of Russia. It also served a useful purpose in rallying support for the new regime during the first critical months after the takeover. And when it turned out that the subsequent attempts to introduce a planned economy more compatible with the ideological platform of the Bolsheviks had only made bad things worse, Lenin was pragmatic enough to make yet another *volte-face* by proclaiming a New Economic Policy (NEP). This reintroduced a fair amount of capitalism and market economy in industry as well as agriculture – a policy finally abandoned by Stalin, who embarked on a ruthless campaign against successful rural entrepreneurs, the so called *kulaks,*[7] accompanied by a brutal programme of collectivization of agricultural land in 1927.

*

There is in fact a very strong case to be made for the notion that it was the peasantry and not the working class that constituted the revolutionary force of predominantly rural Eastern Europe before, during and immediately after the First Word War. Agrarian movements, at least some of which had a distinct Messianic ring to them, played an important role in the early modern history of Bulgaria and Romania – which had enjoyed formal independence since 1878 – as well as in the history of peripheral successor states like Estonia, Latvia, Lithuania, Poland, Hungary and to some extent even in a partially industrialized and developed country like Czechoslovakia. Even in Russia, Lenin was confronted with the untimely success of the social revolutionaries in the April elections of 1917 to the constitutional assembly. Campaigning on a platform of utopian ideas derived from *narodniki* ideology, this movement held out the *obchina*, i.e. the village community, as the basis of Russian society. The representation of this anti-urban, anti-industrial and profoundly nationalist movement in the Constitutional Assembly reduced the socialist factions to a clear-cut minority position.

In Bulgaria, the Agrarian Union (BAU) of Alexandr Stamboliisky dominated the pre- and post-war political stage with its call for land reform and social equality (Bankowicz 1994b, 219–21). In Romania of the early 1920s, there was a populist movement extolling traditional rural values (Dellenbrant 1994b, 205–8; Gilberg 1992, 284–9). Poland had a peasant party with early ambitions to play the leading role that the communists tended to perceive as their historical birth right (Grzybowski 1994a). Hungary was confronted with agrarian socialism at an early stage (Helmreich 1975, 12) and the Smallholders' Party was to remain one of the dominant political forces throughout the inter-war era (Grzybowski 1994b). Similar comments apply to the Agrarian Party of Czechoslovakia (Bankowicz 1994a, 144) and to the agrarian parties of the Baltic states (Dellenbrant 1994a, 78–84).

Some of these movements were what Rokkan (1975) would have called parties of the rural defence; others had a more distinct class profile. The former had a tendency to be reactionary in the sense that they held out a distant and often idealized past as a model for the future, while the latter tended to be radical in the sense that they questioned and challenged the established social order in the country-side as well as in the cities. In the rural environment the landed gentry served as a prime target. In the urban environment it was the cosmopolitan character of a trans-cultural *bourgeoisie* with strong German and Jewish elements that served as scapegoats in the crude agrarian rhetoric and provided a link between radical nationalism and radical agrarianism. In the final analysis, however, all the agrarian movements were inspired by the belief that the solution to the agrarian problem was a *sine qua non* for social peace and harmony; and there is little doubt that the integration of the peasantry represented as serious a challenge to the fledgling parliamentary democracies that were proclaimed throughout Central and Eastern Europe in the wake of the First World War as the integration of the working class.

*

With the benefit of hindsight, it may be argued that the middle strata also played an important role in the destabilization of the fledgling democracies. This is in fact a recurrent theme in Marxist literature, where the rise of fascism and Nazism[8] in the 1920s and 1930s is portrayed as the revolt of the middle class in the face of economic crisis. This is a respectable and plausible argument, particularly in the German case, but it is only one explanation out of many. As will be argued at some length in the following chapter on Central and Eastern Europe during the inter-war era, there is a very strong case to be made for the notion that Germany was a deviant case in the Central and East European context. The macro-sociological perspective applied in fact strongly suggests that Germany should have been one of the few survivor cases in the inter-war struggle between democracy and dictatorship in Central and Eastern Europe.

Notes

1. There were those like Anatole Leroy–Beaulieu (quoted by Tilly 1993), who predicted the breakdown of tsarism even prior to the revolution of 1905 and those like Masaryk (quoted by Kann 1977a) who predicted the demise of the Austro-Hungarian empire. But there was nobody with enough imagination to foresee the breakdown of the entire Central European structure of states.
2. Poland and Lithuania had distant but glorious pasts as independent entities. Finland, Estonia and Latvia were culturally distinct, but had never been independent prior to the inter-war era. Czechoslovakia and Yugoslavia were entirely new state formations.
3. The Croatian Estates fought an up-hill battle against the Hungarian Crown to preserve Latin as the official language of communication between Budapest and Agram (Zagreb).

4. The pan-German programme of 1882 called for Austria to strengthen its German character by giving up supremacy over mainly Slav territories like Galicia and Dalmatia. The ties with Germany were also to be promoted. The pan-Slav movement which was encouraged by St Petersburg called for the union of or at least cooperation among all nations of Slav nationality. The Yugoslav or southern Slav movement called for cooperation among all the Southern Slav nationalities.

5. As demonstrated by Popper (1947), Marx's argumentation in favour of the classless utopia was a three-stage affair. Departing from the economic laws of supply and demand in a state of unrestrained capitalism, he concluded that the rich would become fewer as well as richer, while the poor would become poorer and more and more numerous. Such social polarization would result in social unrest and eventually in a social revolution by the numerically superior working class which would lay the foundations for the classless society.

6. The terms derive from the internal rhetoric of the Russian socialist movement, where Lenin's followers claimed to represent the majority or the many – the Bolsheviks – as opposed to the minority or the few, i. e. the Mensheviks.

7. This term was originally reserved for prosperous, independent farmers, who were branded as capitalist exploiters by the regime, but in the final analysis it turned out to be used indiscriminately and arbitrarily to dispose of actual as well as potential enemies of state (Parland 1993).

8. There is admittedly a case to be made for including fascism and Nazism among the Messianic movements, but in our opinion it is questionable whether this would be appropriate. The Italian and German versions of right-wing totalitarianism advocated the subordination of the individual to the collective cause much like the Soviet communists, who emphasized the primacy of the party as opposed to the *state* or *das Volk*, the favourite objects of identification in the fascist and Nazi rhetoric. But the fascists and Nazis did not have any long term objectives except possibly a constant struggle for *Lebensraum* and the idolization of action as such.

References

Bankowicz, Marek (1994a), 'Czechoslovakia: From Masaryk to Havel', in Sten Berglund and Jan Åke Dellenbrant, eds, *The New Democracies in Eastern Europe: Party Systems and Political Cleavages*, 2nd edition, Aldershot, Edward Elgar.
— (1994b), 'Bulgaria: The Continuing Revolution', in Sten Berglund and Jan Åke Dellenbrant, eds, *opus cited*.
Craig, Gordon A. (1978, 1983), *Deutsche Geschichte 1866–1945: Vom Norddeutschen Bund bis zum Ende des Dritten Reiches*, München, C. H. Beck Verlag.
— (1974, 1995), *Geschichte Europas 1815–1980: Vom Wiener Kongress bis zur Gegenwart*, München, C. H. Beck Verlag.
Crankshaw, Edward (1963, 1994), *The Fall of the House of Habsburg*, London and Basingstoke, Macmillan.
Dellenbrant, Jan Åke (1994a), 'The Re-Emergence of Multi-Partyism in the Baltic States', in Sten Berglund and Jan Åke Dellenbrant, eds, *opus cited*.
— (1994b), 'Romania: The Slow Revolution', in Sten Berglund and Jan Åke Dellenbrant, eds, *opus cited*.
Deutsch, Karl W. (1963), *The Nerves of Government: Models of Political Communication and Control*, New York, Free Press.

Eisenstadt, Schmul N. (1963), *The Political Systems of Empires*, London, Macmillan.

Gilberg, Trond (1992), 'The Multiple Legacies of History: Romania in the Year 1990', in Joseph Held, ed., *The Columbia History of Eastern Europe in the Twentieth Century*, New York, Columbia University Press.

Grzybowski, Marian (1994a), 'Poland: Towards Overdeveloped Pluralism', in Sten Berglund and Jan Åke Dellenbrant, eds, *opus cited*.

— (1994b), 'The Transition to Competitive Pluralism in Hungary', in Sten Berlund and Jan Åke Dellenbrant, eds, *opus cited*.

Helmreich, Ernst C. ed. (1975), *Hungary*, New York and London, Atlantic Books.

Immerfall, Stefan (1992), *Territorium und Wahlverfahren: Zur Modellierung geopolitischer und geoökonomischer Prozesse*, Opladen, Leske & Budrich.

Jászi, Oscar (1929, 1961), *The Dissolution of the Habsburg Monarchy*, London, The University of Chicago Press.

Johnson, Paul (1994), *Modern Times: A History of the World from the 1920s to the 1990s*, London, Orion Books Ltd.

Kann, Robert A. (1950, 1977a), *The Multinational Empire: Nationalism and National Reform in the Habsburg Monarchy*, Vol. I, New York, Octagon Books.

— (1977b), *The Multinational Empire: Nationalism and National Reform in the Habsburg Monarchy*, Vol. II, New York, Octagon Books.

— (1974, 1980), *A History of the Habsburg Empire 1526–1918*, Berkeley, University of California Press.

Kjellén, Rudolf (1921), *Die Grossmächte und die Weltkrise*, Leipzig and Berlin.

Klingemann, Hans-Dieter (1994), 'Die Entstehung wettbewerbsorientierter Parteiensysteme in Osteuropa', WZB, Berlin.

Lenin, Vladimir I. (1905, 1963), *What Is to Be Done*, Oxford, Clarendon Press.

Parland, Thomas (1993), *The Rejection in Russia of Totalitarian Socialism and Liberal Democracy: A Study of the Russian New Right*, Helsinki, The Finnish Society of Sciences and Letters.

Popper, Karl (1947), *The Open Society and Its Enemies*, Vol. 2, London, Routledge.

Rokkan, Stein (1975), 'Dimensions of State Formation and Nation-Building: A Possible Paradigm for Research on Variations within Europe', in Charles Tilly, ed., *The Formation of National States in Europe*, Princeton, Princeton University Press.

'Romania' (1994), in Microsoft Encarta, Microsoft Corporation copyright, Funk & Wagnall's Corporation.

Tilly, Charles (1993), *Die Europäischen Revolutionen*, München, C. H. Beck Verlag.

2. From Formal Democracy to Strong-man Rule: 1917–45

An Experiment in Democracy

The states which emerged out of the peace process in Brest–Litovsk, Versailles, Neuilly and Trianon fell considerably short of being homogeneous nation-states (figure 2.1). With small core populations and sizable ethnic minorities, Czechoslovakia and Yugoslavia were in fact miniature Habsburg empires of sorts. In Czechoslovakia and Yugoslavia, the core populations – sweepingly defined as Czechoslovak and Serbo-Croat nationalities in the 1921 censuses – accounted for 65.5 and 74.3 per cent respectively (Crampton and Crampton 1996). A more narrow and – as we see it – more accurate definition counting only Czechs and Serbs as part of the two core populations would reduce these figures dramatically. With a population of well over 22 million, the Poles had a solid majority in the new Poland, but they had to co-exist with large ethnic minorities – some 5 million Ukrainians, one and a half million Belorussians, 700 000 Germans and Europe's largest Jewish settlement (Grzybowski 1994a).[1] Hungary was considerably closer to the original nation-state model, but only as a result of the humiliating Peace Treaty of Trianon which had transferred millions of ethnic Hungarians into diaspora in neighbouring Romania, Czechoslovakia and Yugoslavia.

All this created a climate of nationalism and ethnic tensions in the entire East European region. In Eastern Europe the inter-war era was in fact anything but peaceful. In 1919–21, Poland waged a successful war against Russia which was to determine its eastern borders until 1939. In October 1920, Polish troops crossed the border of recently independent Lithuania and incorporated the city of Vilnius and the surrounding area into Poland. A little more than two years later, in January 1924, the Lithuanians occupied and annexed the German city

Figure 2.1 European borders as of 1919

of Memel – subsequently known as Klaipeda – which had remained in the custody of the League of Nations after the First World War. In 1938–39, when Czechoslovakia was reeling under the impact of heavy-handed German pressure, Poland and Hungary happily grabbed whatever they could. The Poles occupied the city of Teschen in northern Slovakia and the Hungarians integrated southern Slovakia and Southern Ruthenia into Hungary. A few years later, in 1941, Hungary – then in coalition with Nazi Germany – had actually regained more than half of the territories lost at Trianon (Crampton and Crampton 1996). Yugoslavia was plagued by open ethnic conflicts, mainly between Serbs and Croats, throughout the entire inter-war era, but the Balkan region was also under the sway of great power aspirations as evidenced by Italy's military campaign and the subsequent annexation of Albania.

Figure 2.2 Changes in the Central and East European state systems after the First World War

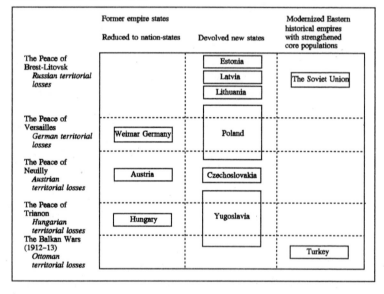

With the exception of Lithuania's war with Poland and the subsequent annexation of Memel, the ethnically homogeneous Baltic countries remained on the outskirts of the international conflicts in Eastern Europe until the Soviet Union set out to incorporate them into the Soviet empire in the late 1930s and early 1940s; and like the other states built on the ruins of the German, Austro-Hungarian, Russian or Ottoman empires they pledged themselves to democracy. The mood was ebullient and full of optimism. But, 20 years after the proclamation of democracy in Central and Eastern Europe democratic optimism had been replaced by a conception of democracy as a beleaguered form of government in this part of the world, clinging as it were to the Atlantic rim.[2] All the states of Central and Eastern Europe, with the exceptions of Switzerland and Czechoslovakia had fallen prey to various forms of authoritarian and totalitarian rule.

Four quite obvious questions may be raised on the basis of this rather elementary observation. What impact did the inter-war experience have on the states of Central and Eastern Europe during the short democratic interlude (1945–49) between Nazi and communist dictatorship? What impact, if any, did the inter-war experience have on the communist regimes that emerged in Eastern and Central Europe in the late 1940s and early 1950s? To what extent can the inter-war experience be said to have any relevance in the present situation? And last, but not least, to what extent can this past crisis of democracy be explained or understood in terms of macro-oriented structural theories?

The impact of the inter-war era on the short democratic parenthesis of 1945–49 and the drawn-out communist interlude of 1949–89 in Eastern and Central Europe will be topics of separate chapters in this volume. The question about the relevance of the inter-war experiment in democracy for contemporary Eastern and Central Europe cannot be empirically answered; it calls for speculation. But if we arrive at some satisfactory structural models when exploring the last question, some implications of relevance for the contemporary scene may still be derived. This is the task towards which we now turn.

There are several theories at hand. When choosing Stein Rokkan's well known conceptual map of Europe (Rokkan 1975; Rokkan and Urwin 1983) as a starting point for our exploration into inter-war Eastern and Central Europe, we do so precisely because it represents an endeavour at a high level of abstraction and generality, just as our study will have to be.

Stein Rokkan's seminal conceptual map of Europe was an attempt to integrate crises in state- and nation-building processes with conditions for democratic survival such as the extension of citizenship rights and the establishment of stable political cleavages in the parliamentary and electoral arenas. Another important and more recent contribution is the notion that the accumulation of crises within a short time span in itself may be detrimental to the survival of a democratic regime. We will refer to this phenomenon as agglutination. On the face of it, agglutination would seem to be particularly suitable for the study of inter-war Central and Eastern Europe which remained affected by an accumulation of challenges of almost the same magnitude as before the war (see chapter 1). The states that emerged out of the various peace treaties shortly before, during and immediately after the First World War satisfied some of, but by no means all, the national grievances which had built up under imperial rule (figure 2.2). Post-war Yugoslavia, Czechoslovakia and Poland actually faced an awesome mixture of nationalist, territorial and Messianic challenges which had serious domestic and foreign policy repercussions. Our basic proposition in this chapter would in fact be that this agglutination of challenges in the aftermath of the European wars of the early 20th century goes a long way towards accounting for the breakdown of the fledgling democratic regimes of Central and Eastern Europe in the 1920s and 1930s.

Giovanni Sartori's distinction between moderate versus extreme pluralism is also part and parcel of an agglutination theory (Sartori 1966, 1976). Sartori's concern about the *Weimarization* of states with highly fragmented party systems strikes a deep chord with the scepticism within the political science community about the survival of democracy in Eastern and Central Europe today.

This fear must be contrasted to the Anglo-Saxon developmental optimism as evidenced by, for example, Almond's and Verba's belief in stable democratic development (Almond and Verba 1980; Almond and Powell 1978; Powell 1982; Huntington 1968). One may even refer to this developmental optimism as a form of Anglo-American ethnocentric bias – a bias also shared by Woodrow Wilson, one of the chief architects of the European inter-war borders.

Another bias, prominent in the literature, is the rather simplistic juxtaposition of 'state' and 'nation'. Rokkan's analytical scheme goes beyond this. He points out that in solving the crises of state- and nation-building, regimes may break down, but they may also be consolidated. If this were not the case, we could not understand the political contrasts between structurally similar pairs such as Bosnia and Switzerland, the Netherlands and Northern Ireland or, for that matter, between Austria and Czechoslovakia.

But Rokkan's framework is marked by a third bias. His conceptual map ends where the Iron Curtain began. He mainly draws on the experience of 18 West and Central European states (Rokkan 1975, 578–9). The following discussion about the survival of democracy in inter-war Europe should be also seen as an attempt to minimize or at least reduce the impact of these three biases.

A Revised Conceptual Map of Europe

Rokkan identifies two dimensions as the basis of his conceptual map of Europe:

> An East-West axis; based on the strength of city networks and political centre formation, and

> A North-South axis; based on the integration of state and church – strong in the Protestant North and weak in the Catholic South (Rokkan and Urwin 1983, 30).

The core of the East–West dimension is a symmetrical triad of states. In the centre, we have city-belt states characterized by strong commercial city networks and weak political centres, surrounded by Eastern and Western empire states, characterized by strong political centres and weak commercial city networks. The city belt is centred on an axis running from Venice to Flanders across the Alps and along the Rhine.[3]

As far as the Western empire states are concerned, we will retain Rokkan's original classification. Denmark, Britain, France and Spain epitomize early and strong European state formation. At the same time all these states became centres of vast overseas empires.

Rokkan's concept of Eastern empire states is too general for our purposes for two reasons. First, it may be argued that parts of these territories include city-belts of considerable importance. The role of the Danube for the Austro-Hungarian empire (and for the Ottoman empire until 1878), the importance of the river system for the development of Russia from Novgorod to Kiev and the importance of the Baltic cities and the Hanseatic League for the development of Prussia–Germany are all cases in point.

Secondly, it may be argued that these territorial units were primarily integrated as early landlocked empires (cf. figure 2.3), and that state-building as such was secondary to the empire formation. A territorial classification of empires must take into consideration imperial aspirations and confrontation as a primary criterion. As for Prussia–Germany and Austria–Hungary, we will retain Rokkan's concept of Eastern empire states. They were built up militarily over the centuries to defend Europe against incursions from the Eurasian steppes. Nevertheless both of these defence systems went through a

Figure 2.3 Democratic survival: a conceptual map

Religious heritage	Late, devolved Western periphery states	Early states formed in the cores of Western seaward empires	City-belt Europe	States based on former core nations of Central European empire states	Late, devolved states from Central European empire states	Late, devolved states from Eastern historical empires	Eastern external historical empires
Protestant countries	Norway Prot.	Denmark, Great Britain Prot.		Sweden Prot.	Finland Prot.	Estonia, Latvia Prot.	
Mixed or substantially secularized countries	(Ulster) Prot./Cath.	France Cath./Sec.	The Netherlands, Switzerland Prot./Cath. Belgium Cath./Sec.	Germany Prot./Cath.	Czechoslovakia (Bohemia, Moravia) Cath./Sec.	(Ukraine) Orth./Cath./Sec.	Russia (S.U.) Orth./Sec.
Counter-reformation countries & non-secularized Orthodox countries	Eire Cath.	Spain, Portugal Cath.		Austria, Hungary Cath.	(Slovakia), Italy, (Slovenia, Croatia) Cath.	Lithuania, Poland Cath. Romania, Bulgaria, Yugoslavia (Serbia) Orth.	
Muslim countries						Albania (Bosnia, Kosovo) (Bulgarian muslim minority) Mus./Sec.	Turkey Mus./Sec.

considerable state-building experience at least with respect to their core territories. The German term *Mark* covers this concept well and Rokkan's term 'empire states' picks up this dimension.

Thr Russian and the Ottoman empires we will basically consider external with aspirations to expand into Europe.[4] As stated in chapter 1, these systems were closer in structure to Eisenstadt's concept of historical empires (Eisenstadt 1963), where the concept of statehood is indeed relegated to a subordinate position. In figure 2.3 we therefore refer to the Russian and Ottoman empires as Eastern historical empires.

At the rim of the symmetrical conceptual map, Rokkan places Western and Eastern periphery states, characterized by weak political centres and late statehood. The concept of Eastern periphery states, needless to say, will be meaningless within our revised framework, since the external historical empires represent Europe's eastern border. Instead we will employ the term 'devolved states' to the territories that gained statehood in the historical process of dismantling the empires from 1878 to 1919.[5] Two types of Eastern devolved states may be distinguished: those devolved from the empire states, after the peace treaty of Versailles, and those devolved from the historical empires after the Balkan wars and the peace treaties of Brest-Litovsk and Versailles (cf. figures 2.2 and 2.3).

The North–South axis in Rokkan's framework is based on the religious status of the European territories as they emerged after the peace treaties of Westphalia and Osnabrück in 1648. The importance of this dimension is based on later political events, notably the conflict between state and church over control of the school system during the 19th century. Needless to say, Rokkan's three-way classification of countries as Protestant, mixed or secularized Catholic and counter-reformation, is too limited for an all European framework. We will include Orthodox as well as Muslim areas in our revised version, while retaining the crucial distinction in terms of integration or lack thereof between state and church. The net result is a fourfold classification of countries according to the relative political autonomy of the religious hierarchy.

As for the Protestant countries, particularly the Lutheran Evangelical, we would argue that they represent total integration and subordination of religious leadership to the state. In the mixed Protestant and Catholic countries as well as the substantially secularized Catholic and Orthodox countries, we would argue that the autonomy from religion has given the state the upper hand, albeit that church interests exist with a potential for independent political influence on the citizens. In the counter-reformation Catholic countries as well as in the non-secularized Orthodox countries, most notably those ecclesiastically affiliated with the Patriarchy of Constantinople, we will argue that there is a potential for dualism between religious and secular authority. It should be noted that this potential is higher in the counter-reformation countries than in the non-secularized Orthodox countries. In the latter, the potential for direct independent church opposition to the state is on the weak side, but it is enhanced by traditional ties often of a clientelistic nature. The last category comprises the Muslim countries. In these areas, secularization is at direct odds with religion. Indeed in modern Turkey this may be considered a major political and social cleavage. The possibility of coexistence between secularized political forces and fundamentalist Muslims within the same regime is very much in doubt – conflicts which will tend to have consequences for the regime.

The application of the above criteria results in a revised conceptual map of inter-war Europe (figure 2.4). The countries and areas appearing in italics have the common denominator that democratic regimes established in the early 1920s did not survive the inter-war period. With their commitment to parliamentary democracy and their vulnerability to the vicissitudes of extreme multi-partyism, the constitutions of Estonia, Latvia, Lithuania (Dellenbrant 1994a) and Poland (Grzybowski 1994a) were inspired by the German Weimar Republic and the Third French Republic. The breakdown came in the form of a series of coups and military take-overs: in Poland by Marshal Józef Piłsudski in May 1926; in Lithuania by Antanas Smetona again in 1926; in Estonia by Prime Minister Konstantin Päts in 1934; in Latvia by Prime Minister Kārlis Ulmanis also in 1934. Hungary experienced parliamentary democracy for a short period after the breakdown of Béla Kun's ill-fated Soviet Republic on 1 August 1919, but the democratic government was overthrown by Admiral Horthy who made himself temporary regent, pending the selection of a royal family (Heinrich 1986, 21–2). The Hungarian case is extreme, but not atypical for the turbulent state of affairs in Eastern Europe in the aftermath of the First World War. With a democratic experience of three years under Stamboliisky in 1920–23, Bulgaria actually stands out as one of the leading democracies in the Balkan area. The royal coups of Romania (1920) and Yugoslavia (1929) are well known (Dellenbrant 1994b). The development towards authoritarianism and totalitarianism in the remaining italicized countries – Austria, Germany, Italy, Spain, Portugal and Greece (Zink 1992) – demonstrates that the breakdown of democracy was by no means a purely East European phenomenon.

Reading the conceptual map diagonally from the south-east corner to the north-west corner, we observe that the chances of democratic survival improve. From the above discussion of some of the cases, it is clear that there are considerable variations in the forms of transition to authoritarianism and totalitarianism in the countries where democracy broke down. Nevertheless, the conceptual map also seems to indicate that the two macro-dimensions of the framework have an impact. A pattern clearly emerges. The dimensions of Rokkan's original conceptual map as well as those of our own revised version, are complex and composite. We obviously need to take a closer look at the two dimensions in order to further clarify the pattern of democratic breakdown and survival.

Two Crucial Dichotomies: State-Building and Secularization

An essential distinction has to be made between those European states with a historical tradition of state-building and those states which primarily had remained empires – or parts thereof – until the First World War. Almost all the states included in Rokkan's original conceptual map belong to the former category. In our framework the states exposed to state-building include the Western periphery states, the Western empire states, the city belt states, the Eastern defence empire states and the states devolved from the Eastern defence empire states after 1918. Despite the fact that the Eastern defence empire states have a strong element of imperial identity, we will nevertheless argue that certainly Sweden and Prussia–Germany, but also Austria-Hungary, at least for their Austrian and Hungarian core populations, had experienced considerable state- and nation-building prior to the First World War (see chapter 1). On the other hand, it will be remembered that the external Russian and Ottoman historical empires had experienced much more limited state-building efforts on the part of their rulers. We will argue that the states, which had devolved from these empires since the latter part of the 19th century, shared this lack of state-building tradition.

On the basis of the above discussion, we have dichotomized the East–West dimension (see figure 2.4). One category of states has a shared experience of Roman law, state-building and relatively early national revival. We have labelled this group of states *the Charlemagne heritage*, since most of them have been influenced by the existence of the Holy Roman empire in the early Middle Ages. The other group of states, known as the 'external challengers', consists of those countries that do not share these traditions and have belonged to the Russian or Ottoman empires. It is tempting to add that they also share a common Byzantine heritage – the strength of which varies with the relative importance of Orthodoxy. Moreover, the lack of a strong state apparatus and the retention of traditional feudal controls made it possible for ancient local authority relationships such as kinship and clientelism to survive to a greater extent than elsewhere in Europe. This tendency was – and remains – more pronounced in the South than in the North.

Figure 2.4 Democratic survival: a classification of European countries in inter-war Europe (short-lived and semi-independent state formations are parenthesized)

Religious autonomy from state authority	State-building tradition	
	The city belt, empire states and states devolved from these empire states: *The Charlemagne heritage*	External eastern historical empires and states devolved from these historical empires: *The external challengers*
Predominantly Protestant countries: *State and Church integrated* **&**	Denmark Sweden Norway Finland Great Britain The Netherlands Switzerland *Germany*	*Estonia* *Latvia*
Secularized Catholic or Orthodox countries: *Dominant state*	France Belgium Czechoslovakia	*Russia (USSR)* *(Ukraine)*
Catholic counter-reformation countries, non-secularized Orthodox countries and Muslim countries: *Continued dualism between state and church/Ecclesia*	Eire *Spain* *Portugal* *Austria* *Hungary* *Italy* *(Croatia)* *(Slovakia)*	*Lithuania* *Poland* *Romania* *Bulgaria* *Yugoslavia (Serbia)* *Greece* *Albania* *Turkey*

Therefore, the North–South dimension has also been dichotomized. We consider the strength and autonomy of political authority vis-à-vis religious leadership to be essential. Religious autonomy is *not* important as such, but its consequences are in the sense that religious autonomy provides a platform legitimizing the attacks on the regime by the counter-movements. The first group of countries includes the Protestant states and the substantially secularized states. The former could even use servants of the church in order to strengthen the bureaucracy, whereas the latter successfully managed to isolate religious interests from governance. The second group comprises the predominantly Catholic states of the counter-reformation, the non-secularized Orthodox states and the Muslim countries and areas. In the case of the Catholic countries, the conflicting influences of State and *Ecclesia* are obvious. In the non-secularized Orthodox and in the Muslim countries, secularization within the regime proved almost impossible during the *ancien régime*. Secularization in Russia and Turkey could only take place after Lenin and Atatürk respectively had overthrown the old regimes. In these countries secularization rather served to strengthen Messianism and other non-democratic options much in the same way that religion had legitimized traditional authoritarianism during the old regimes.

When we sort the countries and areas according to the two dichotomies a very clear pattern emerges. All the countries that remained democratic at the outset of the Second World War belong in one cell. They share *the Charlemagne heritage* and they are all either Protestant or substantially secularized. Eire, which is a counter-reformation country, stands out as the only exception. Moreover one important country, Germany, had developed into a fascist dictatorship despite its solid position in the group of Protestant/secularized countries with a state-building tradition.

The common factors conducive to democratic survival in the inter-war period seem to be closely associated with state-building and state autonomy. In a sense, Max Weber (1978) would hardly have been surprised at this finding given his emphasis on the close association between the consolidation of state authority through the monopoly of legitimate violence on the one hand and the relative autonomy of the bureaucracy on the other hand, as twin bases for a rational form of government. In relation to Rokkan's original emphasis on internal differentiation based in city-structures, our analysis highlights the common state-building and cultural traditions derived from Roman

Law, secularized power, a strong bureaucratic apparatus and legitimized national identity. These factors are by no means absent in Rokkan's work, but our results may suggest that an even more immediate connection exists between successful state- and nation-building on the one hand and successful democratic regimes on the other. It is tempting to employ Weber's old concept of rationality.

Macro Context versus Internal Factors

The contrast to much of the existing literature with its emphasis on internal and contemporary factors is rather stunning. To some extent, this can be accounted for by the preponderance of case studies rather than comparative works. But, as mentioned earlier, a number of comparative theories also exists mainly emphasizing internal factors. Agglutination theories are cases in point. If we apply for example Sartori's theory to our framework, one would expect at least as a good a fit as we have obtained.

In an early article – which comes closer to theory building than most contributions within this field – Sartori (1966) identifies a number of factors that may make the difference between the moderate kind of pluralism conducive to stability and the extreme kind of pluralism conducive to instability:

- the timing of the franchise (the extension of the suffrage)
- the timing of proportional representation (PR)
- the number of cleavages
- the structure of cleavages
- the degree of party organization

The logic is simple and straightforward. A rapid process of democratization results in extreme multi-partyism. The political market is literally flooded with new political entrepreneurs hoping for parliamentary representation. PR leads to a low parliamentary threshold and serves as yet another incentive for hopeful political entrepreneurs. The sooner it is introduced, the more likely it is to contribute towards extreme multi-partyism. The more dimensions of conflict there are in a society and the more complex a cleavage structure it has, the more likely it is that it will serve as a *niche* for a large number of political parties; and finally, the more poorly organized the political parties are, the more room there would seem to be for additional political parties. A low level of mass mobilization – as evidenced by a low degree of party organization and, for that matter, by a low turnout on election day – serves as a yet another incentive for the hopeful political entrepreneurs.

And on the other hand, a slow process of democratization makes for moderate multi-partyism, perhaps even for the British kind of two-party politics. Majority representation serves as a barrier against extreme multi-partyism and the longer majority representation is retained, the more likely it is that the party system will become moderate. The fewer cleavages there are in a society and the simpler its cleavage structure remains, the less room there is for the extreme kind of multi-party politics; and last, but not least, the better organized the established political parties are, the less leeway there is for new political entrepreneurs in the political arena. A high level of mass mobilization serves as a deterrent against fragmentation of the party system.

When we apply Sartori's model in a crude way to our fourfold table, it is readily seen that the agreement is less than perfect. Czecho-slovakia, a clear-cut case of agglutination with a highly fragmented party system and a truly complicated cleavage structure including social and ethnic conflicts, features prominently among our survivor cases, while less clear-cut cases of agglutination like Austria and Hungary stand out as indisputable breakdown cases. Similar comments apply to Finland,[6] yet another potential breakdown case according to Sartori, but a strong candidate for survival by the logic inherent in our classification scheme.

The Third Factor: Structural and Practical Cooptation

Our discussion of the Central and East European countries in the inter-war era makes it abundantly clear that Sartori's model does not work. Our framework would seem to perform somewhat better, but it too fails to account for two of the cases, Germany and Eire. According to our model, democracy should have survived in Germany and should not have survived in Eire.

We would propose that a third factor be added to the analysis in order to account for the deviations: the integration of cleavages through meso-level cooptation. Two forms of cooptation are well documented in the literature: structural cooptation in the form of various types of consociational devices and practical cooptation in the form of broadening the base of the regime by including the elites of groups representing cleavages hitherto excluded from power. Such consociational devices are in fact prominent in Arend Lijphart's (1980) attempt to account for the democratic stability of contemporary West European countries with complex cleavage structures and party systems like Belgium, the Netherlands and Switzerland. The emphasis is on institutional structures that make it possible for elites, representing all relevant cleavages to influence governmental decisions, regardless of whether they are in government or not. These structures thus provide a platform for elite cooptation. More recently, O'Donnell, Schmitter and Whitehead (1986) have drawn attention to the importance of practical cooptation of elites within the framework of their research on the transition to democracy on the Iberian Peninsula in the 1970s. The emphasis is on informal fora for discourse among elites and the development of a basic understanding of the rules of the game, as opposed to the institutional structures which are crucial in Lijphart's theory.[7]

Our basic argument is that successful completion of state-building and clear autonomy from religious authority were not sufficient to make a state safe for democracy in the inter-war period. The survival of democracy also requires that the elites of all or most relevant cleavages be integrated into governance or into a position of strong influence upon the government.

The survivors explained by our model in figure 2.4 are all cases either of structural or practical cooptation of major social elites. Structural cooptation is well known in the Netherlands: the great compromise of 1917 and *verzuiling* (Lijphart 1968); in Belgium: the *familles spirituelles* (Lorwin 1971); in Switzerland: *Proporz* (Lembruch 1967a, 1967b; Dahl 1966; Kerr 1974). Practical cooptation in the form of political compromises are known from Scandinavia: the red–green compromises (Lindström 1985); from Czechoslovakia: the *Pětka* – the Committee of Five (Bradley 1992; Bankowicz 1994a); from Great Britain: the Second World War government of National Unity and Ramsey McDonald's Labour government (McKenzie 1964); from France: Léon Blum's popular front government and the subsequent integration of all parliamentary groups into governmental politics.

Structural cooptation certainly was not unknown in our deviant German case. Thus, the two major parties of the Weimar regime, the Catholic *Zentrum* and the Social Democrats had developed a societal organizational network which had similarities to for example Dutch *verzuiling* (Craig 1978, 499-511). But contrary to the Dutch compromises, the Weimar compromise excluded major forces. The exclusion of communists was maybe not so important as the virtual exclusion of the nationalist, conservative, rural and Eastern political segment. This segment was *not* removed from competitive politics at the polls, but it had little or no incentive to join the constitutional regime compromise. On the contrary, anti-regime sentiment became a progressively more important component in the politics of the right. This withdrawal from the parliamentary bargaining process by a major segment of the country's political and military elite makes Germany different from all the above-mentioned cases of democratic survival. Even so, it is noteworthy that the events leading up Hitler's *Machtergreifung* in 1933 took place, to a large extent, within the procedural framework of the constitution. In our context it deserves to be emphasized that not only Hitler and his followers, but also the president of the Republic and Hitler's two predecessors as chancellor – von Papen and von Schleicher – both represented the segment initially excluded from the institutional structures of the Weimar republic.[8]

Our opposite deviant case – Eire – the only democratic survivor among the non-secularized states, can also be explained by the third factor. In the constitutional compromise which paved the way for the foundation of an Irish Republic, a major segment was excluded, as in Germany. But, unlike Germany, the democratic constitution was not subverted by the nationalists, who, unlike the German National Socialists, had no means whatsoever of redressing their national grievances on their own.[9]

The third factor would thus seem to account for the two deviant cases, Germany and Eire. By the 1930s, German democracy finds itself in a no-win situation with a ruling political elite not committed to the constitutional compromise faced by an opposition even less committed to Weimar. At the same time, Irish democracy is in a no-lose-situation with a governing elite not overwhelmingly committed to the democratic compromise, but repeatedly returned to power at the polls, faced by an opposition whose very existence depends on that very compromise.

But the third factor – structural and practical cooptation – must not be seen as a residual factor accounting only for the two deviant cases. In many of the East European countries, the turbulent events of the early 1920s produced a political climate which resulted in the exclusion of segments from integration into political life. By way of example, it may be mentioned that Béla Kun's aborted revolution in Hungary stigmatized organized labour in Hungarian politics for the duration of the inter-war period (Grzybowski 1994b). In a similar vein, it may be noted that left-wing elites of the Ukrainian and Belorussian minorities found themselves suppressed and excluded due to Warsaw's fear of contagion from Moscow (Crampton and Crampton 1996). In Bulgaria, the coup against the Stamboliisky government in 1923 also served to estrange the left-wing agrarian elites, who were to align themselves with the communists in the uprising of September 1923 (Bankowicz 1994b). In the early 1930s, Hitler's *Machtergreifung* and the Moscow show trials brought about a consolidation of established political forces in order to prevent the extreme left and the extreme right from seizing power in Estonia and Latvia. A similar rhetoric had accompanied the machinations of the royal families of Romania and Yugoslavia.

The Inter-War Era and Beyond

Where the state-building tradition was weak and the legacy of empire strong, or where secular nation-building was still impaired by deeply rooted religious sentiments, or where significant segments representing major cleavages were not coopted into a constitutional compromise, the chances for democratic survival in inter-war Europe were slim indeed.

The impact of our three structural determinants of democratic survival is unquestionable. Strictly speaking, this finding only pertains to the inter-war era, but the implications are nevertheless manifold. To the extent that the relationship between democracy and the three structural determinants is indeed a stable one, we would expect the countries of Central and Eastern Europe to be more or less capable of coping with the communist challenge with which they were gradually confronted in the wake of the Second World War. The communist claim on hegemony was backed by the overpowering presence of the Soviet Red Army and thus hard to refuse, but it could be accepted immediately and with enthusiasm or only reluctantly and with little or no enthusiasm. We would expect Czechoslovakia, the sole inter-war democratic survivor, and late inter-war democratic failures like Poland and Germany to be more reluctant than other Central and East European states to settle within the Soviet mould. In a similar vein, we would expect the Central and East European states with an inter-war record of democracy to be more open to pluralism under communism than Russia's other allies.

But there is also another aspect to the survival of democracy in this region. In the long run, even the most stable macro-sociological relationships are bound to change. The communist parties that were to take over Central and Eastern Europe after the brief semi-democratic interlude of 1945–49 had state-building and socioeconomic change at the very top of the their political agendas; and the primacy of politics, industrialization, urbanization and secularization became the catch-words of the day in the 1950s and 1960s. It would therefore be entirely plausible to draw the somewhat paradoxical conclusion that the prospects for democracy are particularly bright in those former communist states, where the ruling Marxist–Leninist parties were particularly successful in promoting their pet projects.

The third factor, elite cooptation, is more dependent upon the political cultures that are emerging now. Yet, it is no less paradoxical. Some of the traditions for elite cooptation in Eastern Europe and the former Soviet Union are in themselves far from democratic. Clientelism, kinship and corruption are hard to reconcile with democracy, but may nevertheless fulfil a purpose in the progression towards democracy.

Notes

1. Poland had Ukrainian and Belorussian minorities in the range of 15-20 per cent, a Jewish minority of some 10 per cent and a small German minority of 5 per cent.
2. This chapter draws heavily on an article by Frank Aarebrot and Sten Berglund entitled 'Statehood, Secularization, Cooptation: Explaining Democratic Survival in Inter-War Europe – Stein Rokkan's Conceptual Map Revisited'. In Stefan Immerfall and Peter Steinbach, Hrsg., *Historisch-vergleichende Makrosoziologie: Stein Rokkan – der Beitrag eines Kosmopoliten aus der Peripherie*, published as Special Issue No. 2, Vol. 20, of *Historical Social Research*.
3. In a recent paper, focusing on the city belt of the 16th century, Pål Bakka (1994) suggests a revision of Rokkan's conceptual map which ties in neatly with our own proposal (cf. figure 2.3).
4. This classification is somewhat at odds with the Russian national tradition of portraying Russia as a Christian defence empire against yellow and Muslim hordes, as evidenced by such concepts as the Byzantine heritage and Moscow as the third Rome.
5. It may be argued that the dismantling of the Ottoman empire in Europe started with the independence of Greece in 1829. But this process did not gain impetus until the Balkan wars in the latter half of the 19th century.

6. In all fairness, it should be noted that the logic of our own model is contingent upon the original classification and Finland is admittedly a borderline case. In figure 2.4 it was classified as devolved from an Eastern defence empire state, i.e. Sweden, of which Finland was an integral part until the Swedish–Russian War of 1809, rather than as devolved from an Eastern historical empire, i.e. Russia, from which Finland seceded in 1917. In the Finnish process of nation-building prior to formal independence anti-Swedish and anti-Russian sentiments coexisted in the form of rival nationalist movements.

7. This is in fact a central theme in Ulf Lindström's analysis of the failure of the radical right to successfully challenge democracy in Scandinavia during the inter-war era. Lindström shows how socialist elites were coopted into the political system through compromises with already established agrarian elites, the so-called red–green compromises, which protected the Scandinavian countries from a polarization between the radical right and the radical left of the kind that destabilized Weimar Germany.

8. It should be kept in mind that we address ourselves to the survival of democracy as such and not to the emergence of various totalitarian and authoritarian forms of government. We are well aware that to scholars concerned with the rise of fascism, Germany can hardly be considered a deviant case. For an effort to account for the rise of fascism within the framework of a similar comparative conceptual tradition, see Bernt Hagtvet and Stein Rokkan (1980).

9. The nationalist segment under the leadership of Eamon de Valera, which refused to accept the secession of Ulster, was initially not part of the formation of the democratic regime. De Valera's party, *Fionna Faíl*, subsequently came to power within the framework of the constitution and de Valera was elected president of the Republic. *Fionna Faíl* benefitted from the existence of an unresolved national issue, Ulster.

References

Aarebrot, Frank and Sten Berglund, 'Statehood, Secularization, Cooptation: Explaining Democratic Survival in Inter-War Europe – Stein Rokkan's Conceptual Map Revisited', in Stefan Immerfall and Peter Steinbach, Hrsg., *Historisch-vergleichende Makrosoziologie: Stein Rokkan – der Beitrag eines Kosmopoliten aus der Peripherie*, published as Special Issue No. 2, Vol. 20, of *Historical Social Research*.

Almond, Gabriel A. and G. Bingham Powell Jr (1978), *Comparative Politics: A Developmental Approach*, 2nd edition, Boston, Little, Brown.

— and Sidney Verba (1980), *The Civic Culture Revisited*, Boston, Little, Brown.

Bakka, Pål H. (1994), 'Imperial Breakdown, Political Fragmentation and State-Building: An Attempt to Apply Stein Rokkan's Conceptual Map of Europe to the Political Development of Eastern Europe', paper prepared for the *IPSA World Congress in Berlin*, 20–27 August.

Bankowicz, Marek (1994a), 'Czechoslovakia – From Masaryk to Havel', in Sten Berglund and Jan Åke Dellenbrant, eds, *The New Democracies in Eastern Europe: Party Systems and Political Cleavages*, 2nd edition, Aldershot, Edward Elgar.

— (1994b), 'Bulgaria: The Continuing Revolution', in Sten Berglund and Jan Åke Dellenbrant, eds, *opus cited*.

Bradley, John F. N. (1971), *Czechoslovakia*, Edinburgh, Edinburgh University Press.

— (1992), *Czechoslovakia's Velvet Revolution: A Political Analysis*, Cambridge, Cambridge University Press.

Craig, Gordon A. (1978) *Germany: 1866-1945*, Oxford, Clarendon Press.

Crampton, Richard and Ben Crampton (1996), *Atlas of Eastern Europe in the Twentieth Century*, London and New York, Routledge.

Dahl, Robert A. (1966), *Political Oppositions in Western Democracies*, New Haven, Yale University Press.

Dellenbrant, Jan Åke (1994a), 'The Re-Emergence of Multi-Partyism in the Baltic States', in Sten Berglund and Jan Åke Dellenbrant, eds, *opus cited*.

— (1994b), 'Romania: The Slow Revolution', in Sten Berglund and Jan Åke Dellenbrant, eds, *opus cited*.

Eisenstadt, Schmul N. (1963), *The Political Systems of Empires*, London, Macmillan.

Fredriksson, Gunnar (1982), *Det politiska språket*, 6th edition, Malmö, Tiden.

Grzybowski, Marian (1994a), 'Poland – Towards Overdeveloped Pluralism', in Sten Berglund and Jan Åke Dellenbrant, eds, *opus cited*.

— (1994b), 'The Transition to Competitive Pluralism in Hungary', in Sten Berglund and Jan Åke Dellenbrant, eds, *opus cited*.

Hagtvet, Bernt and Stein Rokkan (1980), 'The Conditions of Fascist Victory', in Stein Ugelvik Larsen, B. Hagtvet and J. P. Myklebust, eds, *Who Were the Fascists?*, Bergen, Universitetsforlaget.

Heinrich, Hans Georg (1986), *Hungary: Politics, Economics and Society*, London, Pinter.

Huntington, Samuel P. (1968), *Political Order in Changing Societies*, New Haven, Yale University Press.

Kerr, Henry H. Jr (1974), *Switzerland: Social Cleavages and Partisan Conflict*, Beverly Hills, Sage Publications.

Lembruch, Gerhard (1967a), *Proporzdemokratie: Politisches System und Politische Kultur in der Schweiz und Österreich*, Mohr.

— (1967b), 'A Noncompetitive Pattern of Conflict Management in Liberal Democracies: The Case of Switzerland, Austria, Lebanon', paper presented at the 1967 IPSA World Congress.

Lijphart, Arend (1968), *The Politics of Accomodation: Pluralism and Democracy in the Netherlands*, Berkeley, University of California Press.

— (1980), Democracy in Plural Societies: A Comparative Exploration, New Haven, Yale University Press.

Lindström, Ulf (1985), *Fascism in Scandinavia in Scandinavia 1920-40*, Stockholm, Almqvist & Wiksell International.

Lorwin, Val (1971), 'Segmented Pluralism: Ideological Cleavages and Political Cohesion in the Smaller European Democracies', *Comparative Politics*, January.

McKenzie, Robert T. (1964), *British Political Parties: The Distribution of Power Within the Conservative and Labour Parties*, London and Tonbridge, Mercury Books.

Moore, Barrington (1967), *The Social Origins of Dictatorship and Democracy*, London, Penguin Books.

O'Donnell, Guillermo, Philippe C. Schmitter and Lawrence Whitehead, eds, (1986), *Transitions from Authoritarian Rule: Prospects for Democracy*, Baltimore, Johns Hopkins University Press.

Powell, G. Bingham Jr (1982), *Contemporary Democracies: Participation, Stability, and Violence*, Cambridge, Mass., Harvard University Press.

Rokkan, Stein (1975), 'Dimensions of State Formation and Nation-Building: A Possible Paradigm for Research on Variations within Europe', in Charles Tilly, ed, *The Formation of National States in Europe*, Princeton, Princeton University Press.

— and Derek Urwin (1983), *Economy, Territory, Identity*, London, Sage.

Sartori, Giovanni (1966), 'European Political Parties: The Case of Polarized Pluralism', in Joseph LaPalombara and Myron Weiner, eds, *Political Parties and Political Development*, Princeton, Princeton University Press.

— (1976), *Parties and Party Systems: A Framework for Analysis*, Cambridge, Cambridge University Press.

Weber, Max (1978), *Economy and Society*, edited by G. Roth and C. Wittich, Berkeley and Los Angeles, University of California Press.

Zink, Allan (1992), 'Political Crisis and Collapse: Greece in the Inter-War Period', paper prepared for the CCC Project.

3. Freedom from Fascism, but How?
Eastern Europe in 1945–49

The Anti-fascist Coalition

The alliance that forced Nazi Germany into unconditional surrender in May 1945 was truly heterogeneous. Great Britain and the United States did not have much in common with the Soviet Union other than a strong desire to wipe out Nazi Germany. In this sense, the alliance between them may be described as an anti-fascist coalition with strongly anti–German overtones. The gradual breakdown of the German war-machine under the impact of the advancing allied forces in the last few months of the war and Germany's subsequent unconditional surrender introduced a new element of tension and discord into a coalition where the individual partners all had a legitimate interest in the spoils. But the defeat of Nazi Germany did not do much to change the anti-fascist thrust of the coalition. Nor did it contribute towards improving the standing of the Germans in the international community. It was rather the other way around.

German occupation had imposed hardship everywhere, but nowhere to such an extent as in the occupied parts of Eastern Europe and the Soviet Union where it had been accompanied by summary executions, ethnic cleansing, slave labour and a variety of other measures in flagrant violation of international law. The full story of what had happened under German rule became public knowledge with the liberation of Eastern Europe by the Soviet Red Army in the autumn of 1944 and the early winter of 1945. This was damaging, but by no means to the same extent as the crimes against the European Jewry, which became generally known with the gradual liberation of the German concentration camps by the allies. The many accounts of life under the German jackboot and the frequent newsreels from the

German death camps served as a reminder of the importance of combatting fascism not only on the battle field and the media thus provided additional fuel to the widespread fears of Germans in general and German nationalism in particular.

This was the intellectual climate that prevailed when Europe's borders were redrawn in the wake of the Second World War (figure 3.1). It is hardly surprising that the borders were changed to the disadvantage of Germany and to the advantage of neighbouring Czechoslovakia, Poland and the Soviet Union. But it is worth noting that the implementation of the border changes had a strong element of retribution attached to it. The 12–15 million inhabitants of Silesia, Pomerania, East Prussia and the *Sudetenland* were literally evicted from their homes and deported to what remained of Germany in operations by the occupying forces which fulfilled all the requirements of ethnic cleansing.

For all intents and purposes, the new borders of Eastern Europe were dictated by the Soviet Union – the only remaining great power in the region – and the Soviet Union also came out of this process as the only net winner. The Baltic states found themselves reincorporated into the Soviet Union after a brief spell of relative autonomy under German tutelage. Romania was deprived of Bessarabia and Bukovina, but was allowed to retain control of predominantly Hungarian Transylvania; and though technically in coalition with the Soviet Union, Czechoslovakia and Poland both had to give in to Russian expansionism.[1] Stalin had no intention whatsoever of giving up his part of what had been gained by the ill-fated Molotov–Ribbentrop Pact between the Soviet Union and Nazi Germany in 1939; and Poland's territorial expansion at Germany's expense was construed as a belated compensation for substantial territorial losses in the east.

*

Territorial changes of this magnitude provide fertile soil for national resentment. But there was little the East Europeans could do about them in the face of the overpowering presence of the Soviet Red Army, which dominated all of Eastern Europe; and though perhaps less than enthusiastic about some aspects of the Russian domination of Eastern Europe, there was little the Western allies could do about it short of driving the Russians out of Eastern Europe by force. And, although perhaps militarily feasible, this was a strategy the allies were

Figure 3.1 Border changes in Europe after 1945

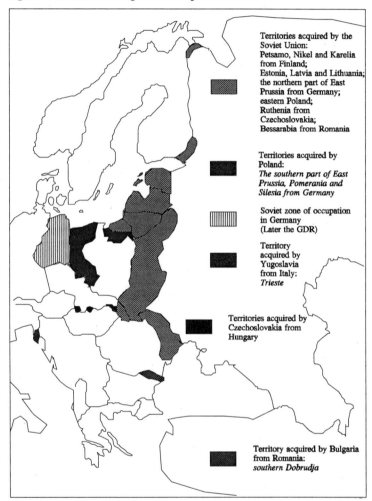

Territories acquired by the
Soviet Union:
Petsamo, Nikel and Karelia
from Finland;
Estonia, Latvia and Lithuania;
the northern part of East
Prussia from Germany;
eastern Poland;
Ruthenia from
Czechoslovakia;
Bessarabia from Romania

Territories acquired by
Poland:
*The southern part of East
Prussia, Pomerania and
Silesia from Germany*

Soviet zone of occupation
in Germany
(Later the GDR)

Territory
acquired by
Yugoslavia
from Italy:
Trieste

Territories acquired by
Czechoslovakia from
Hungary

Territory acquired by Bulgaria
from Romania:
southern Dobrudja

not ready for, at least *not* in the immediate aftermath of the Second
World War. The United States and Britain opted for a strategy of far-
reaching cooperation with their war-time ally who was promoted to a
position of unparalleled prestige in the international community as a

member of the international war-crimes tribunal in Nuremberg and a permanent member of the United Nations' Security Council.

There was widespread acceptance in Great Britain and the United States of the Soviet need to have a sphere of influence in Eastern Europe (Brzezinski 1965, 4–5). The Soviet Union had come out of the war vindicated by its valiant struggle against fascism. Dictatorship was seen as a rightwing and not a leftwing phenomenon. The efforts by the Soviet Union to undermine the political right in general and fascism in particular within the Soviet sphere of interest were hailed as an instalment on democracy even by many commentators and analysts in the United States and Great Britain; and, initially at least, Russia's Western allies had little sympathy or understanding for those prisoners of war who resisted extradition to the Soviet Union (Craig 1978; 1983).

A Revolutionary Situation?

Marxism–Leninism not only has a utopian streak to it (see chapter 1). It also provides excellent guidance for prospective revolutionaries. Lenin, in fact, has more to say about how and when to overthrow the *ancien régime* than about the difficult art of building socialism, to say nothing of communism.[2]   War, economic hardship and inter-elite conflicts are portrayed by Lenin as having a large revolutionary potential. But this is not enough. It also takes a strong revolutionary socialist party which knows how to set the masses in motion without succumbing either to rightwing trade unionism or leftwing sectarianism (Lenin 1905, 1963).

As of 1945, Eastern Europe fulfilled most of these criteria. The region had just come out of a devastating war. War and occupation had brought the East European economies to a standstill. The countries that had fought the war on the losing side like Hungary and Romania found themselves up against massive war reparations to the Soviet Union, which impounded and dismantled one factory after another in the occupied territories (Craig 1978; 1983). The war had taken a heavy toll on the political elites of pre-war Eastern Europe. In Germany the Nazi regime had all but wiped out the pre-war social democratic and communist party organizations. In Poland, which had been divided into a German and a Russian sphere of domination in the wake of the Molotov–Ribbentrop Pact of 1939, there had been no limit to the

Figure 3.2 Soviet Red Army presence in Europe after 1945

political persecution of actual and potential opponents of the war-time new orders. Germany and the Soviet Union both went to great lengths to make sure that Poland would be deprived not only of its incumbent leaders but also of its future potential for national leadership, as evidenced by the Nazi campaign against the Polish intelligentsia and by the summary execution of 15000 (*sic!*) Polish officers in the Katyn forest near Smolensk, by the Soviet security forces (NKVD) in June 1941 (Fowkes 1995, 6). In this respect, Poland was probably more severely hit than the other East European countries, including the Baltic states, which also experienced successive waves of Soviet and German domination.

There is no doubt that the war dealt a serious blow to the political elites in all of Eastern Europe. Large segments of the inter-war elites were forced underground and/or into exile in London or Moscow; and the elites, who had shouldered the responsibility of governing under Nazi tutelage, came out of the war discredited by their collaboration with Germany. The domestic underground did not necessarily see eye to eye with the opposition in exile; the opposition that had opted for a safehaven in London did not necessarily agree with the opposition that had sought refuge in Moscow; and the established political elites who survived the transition from Nazi totalitarianism to political pluralism without being subject to criminal proceedings for high treason or war crimes did not necessarily enjoy the trust and respect of the other potential post-war leaders. The conditions did vary from country to country, but as a rule there was a great potential for inter- and intra-elite strife to be exploited by those with an interest in destabilizing the heterogeneous and fragile political regimes that established themselves in Eastern Europe in 1944-45 as the Germans were driven out of the area.

The Yalta and Potsdam agreements of February and August 1945 between Great Britain, the Soviet Union and the United States foresaw a democratic development under Soviet supervision in Eastern Europe (Berglund and Dellenbrant 1994); and at the outset at least, there were few indications that the entire region would be engaged a frantic look-alike contest with the Soviet Union within a few short years. The Soviet Union had a preference for popular-front governments of all democratic forces, including the re-emerging communist parties. But at this stage the local communists carefully avoided doing anything that might have suggested that they entertained totalitarian ambitions of the Soviet kind; and free or almost free elections were scheduled to take place as soon as the situation had stabilized.

*

The truth of the matter is that the last and crucial component of Lenin's revolutionary model simply was not fulfilled. The vast majority of the local East European communist parties were far too weak and enjoyed far too little popular support to take the lead in what might have been a revolutionary situation. With the exception of the Communist Party of Czechoslovakia, the East European communist parties had a very small constituency and met with a great deal of suspicion. The influx of new supporters from Moscow helped prop them up, but this was a mixed blessing as those who had sat out the war in Moscow tended to be regarded with suspicion in their home countries.

This leaves one revolutionary force not foreseen by Lenin, who had addressed himself to the question of how to overthrow the Tsarist regime in Russia: the Soviet Red Army which was free to pull weight and use strong-armed tactics in an Eastern Europe safely removed from the Western sphere of influence (figure 3.2).[3] It would be wrong to claim that this potential revolutionary agent did not make its presence felt from the very beginning. It certainly did, but the Red Army was not used to coerce the emerging democracies in Eastern Europe into copying the Soviet system of government until 1947-48.

Until that point in time, the Soviet Communist Party made a virtue of the obvious differences between the Soviet Union and the so-called popular democracies in Eastern Europe. The new regimes in Eastern Europe were neither bourgeois democracies of the West European variety, nor socialist democracies of the Soviet type, but something in between. The proletariat had not monopolized the political power, but shared it with other classes and parties. The cooperation across socioeconomic and political boundaries, which was a byproduct of the underground resistance, had survived the war in the shape of a patriotic front, where the local communist party did not command a majority in its own right; and the means of production largely remained in private hands. According to the Communist Party of the Soviet Union, the popular democracies represented a preliminary stage in the progression towards a socialist democracy of the superior Soviet type. The official Soviet attitude is readily apparent from a 1947 article in the *Bolshevik*,[4] the theoretical mouthpiece of the communist party, which is worth quoting at some length:

> There have arisen in these countries new, higher forms of democracy as compared to the old, bourgeois parliamentarian democracy. These

countries have so developed and expanded democracy as to signify the participation of workers and peasants in the state administration and make the benefits of democracy accessible to the broadest masses. Thus new forms of state polity have been created which are a big step forward in comparison to the bourgeois democratic states and which offer possibilities for further progress by these countries in the economic and political fields.

The local East European communists played a similar tune and kept a considerable distance from the Soviet model. In his book, *The Soviet Bloc: Unity and Conflict* (1965), Zbigniew K. Brzezinski, the American sovietologist and political scientist, quotes a number of statements by leading East European communists, which make popular democracy into something quite different from what it became. By way of example, Dimitrov of Bulgaria sided with those demanding constitutional safeguards for private property (*sic!*), while Bierut of Poland came out in favour of harmony between the state, on the one hand, and private enterprise (*sic!*) on the other. And, though pledging allegiance to socialism in general, several of the East European communist leaders went public with the idea that the dictatorship of the proletariat could – and must – be by-passed in Eastern Europe.

From Diversity to Unity

The communist takeover of Eastern Europe is well known and well documented. The sequence of events varies from country to country, but, generally speaking, the East European countries went through a process that literally wiped out the opposition and left the communists firmly in command. The social democrats were prevailed upon to join forces with the communists who were to dominate the newly founded Marxist–Leninist party organizations from the very beginning. The bourgeois or non-socialist parties found themselves exposed to what became known as the *salami* tactics of the ruling communist party and they all had to sacrifice all but the pro-communist left wing in a series of piecemeal purges designed to weed out actual and potential enemies of the state. Some of the bourgeois parties were eventually banned altogether; others survived as trusted coalition partners and allies of the communists within the governing national or popular fronts, but only after they had renounced the idea that the communist hegemony might be reversible. The East European look-alike contest with Moscow of the late 1940s and early 1950s was paralleled by the somewhat absurd competition among the allied parties for support and recognition from the Marxist–Leninist party whose platform they had made into their own pending acceptance as full-fledged members of the ruling party.[5]

At this stage of the transformation process, yet two other frequently quoted prerequisites of liberal democracy were undermined. The freedoms of the press and assembly were concepts that carried little prestige among East European communists keen on transforming their respective societies into mirror images of a supposedly superior Soviet model. Nor did the previous pledge to the virtues of a mixed – as opposed to a planned – economy prevent the East European communist leaders from embarking on a large-scale campaign designed to wipe out private enterprise, including the agricultural sector, when they felt they could do so with impunity.

In the process, the backing of the Soviet Red Army was crucial. It may in fact safely be argued that Eastern Europe would not have turned communist if the local East European communists had not acted in collusion with the Red Army. This is actually a recurrent theme in cold war accounts of the dramatic events as of 1947-49 in Eastern Europe on both sides of the Iron Curtain. Western historians and political scientists refer to the enslavement of the peoples of Eastern Europe by the Soviet Red Army and their Soviet and East European counterparts pay tribute to the liberation of the peoples of Eastern Europe from the yoke of fascism and capitalism by the glorious Red Army. But there is general agreement that the social and political transformation of the East European countries from pluralist democracies to totalitarian communist states within the span of a few short years in the late 1940s and early 1950s could not have been engineered if it had not been for what may neutrally be described as the decisive role of the Soviet Red Army in occupied and liberated countries alike (Berglund 1994).

*

The net result of this process of transformation was a set of countries in Eastern Europe that seemed to have everything in common – the same system of government, the same economic system, the same ideology and the same coalition partners in international affairs. In the following chapter we will argue that this was partly an optical illusion.

The Soviet model was imposed on a number of countries that were basically rather heterogeneous and it did not quite succeed in eradicating the underlying differences. In this chapter we will argue that Eastern Europe could be divided into three, possibly four, groups of countries in the late 1940s and early 1950s. Germany and Czechoslovakia were deviant cases, but for entirely different reasons. Stalin perceived the part of Germany under Soviet occupation as a bargaining chip in the upcoming peace settlement and was in no hurry to introduce the Soviet brand of socialism in East Germany (Fowkes 1995, 24–7). Czechoslovakia came out of the war with strong social democratic and communist (*sic!*) movements with a potential for independent revolutionary action (Bankowicz 1994a). Poland, Hungary, Bulgaria and Romania represent the mainstream in the sense that weak communist parties had to be propped up by the Soviet Union in order to pave the way for a communist regime. And Yugoslavia and Albania were outliers in the sense that they owed their liberation not primarily to the Soviet Red Army but to a domestic underground army capable of setting its own time-table and agenda for the socialist transformation to which it was committed (Fowkes 1995, 44–51).

Germany: Revolution with Delay

'You liberated us. You gave us the revolution which we did not have the strength to make in 1918, nor in 1945. Maybe the gift you gave us was too much for us to handle'. These are the words of Witte – the hero of Stefan Heym's famous novel on the dramatic events of June 1953 when the workers of East Berlin took to the streets against the self-proclaimed workers' government of Walter Ulbricht – in an off-the-record conversation with one of his counterparts in the Soviet military administration for Germany as tensions were building up in East Berlin. 'What should we have done', asks the Russian. 'It is not always possible to wait for the right conditions to materialize.'

*

The above conversation is fictional, but might have been for real. Germany was in no mood for a communist revolution in 1945. The revolution came later, and then only in the Soviet-occupied zone of Germany where it was imposed by the Red Army. In an effort to make sure that the communist party (KPD) would be returned to a position of prominence in German politics, Moscow shipped plane-loads of German communists in exile, including the so-called *Gruppe Ulbricht*, to Berlin within days of Germany's unconditional surrender in May 1945. But the communists were under instructions to lie low and did so to the point of cold-shouldering an early invitation by the organizationally weak social democrats to form a united socialist party. In fact, the KPD did not take the Social Democratic Party (SPD) up on its offer until the autumn of 1945, when the social democrats had started losing interest in the entire venture (Berglund 1994, 120–2).

With the benefit of hindsight, it is readily seen that the communists lost a great deal of momentum by underestimating the ability of the social democrats to re-establish themselves as an independent political force in Germany. This turned the merger of the two parties in a united socialist party (SED) into a rather drawn-out affair, and the open opposition from within the local social democratic associations was not brought under control until the winter of 1945 or early spring of 1946 (Mattedi 1966, 66–73).

In the meantime, however, two new parties had made their entry into the political arena. They were both of the bourgeois variety and catered to the same social groups, the one (CDU) on confessional and the other (LDPD) on general liberal grounds. With their appeal of 26 June 1945, the Christian Democrats were the first ones to get organized. Somewhat unexpectedly, they called for the nationalization of the mines and other 'monopoly-type key enterprises', but they also came out strongly in favour of religion and religious instruction within the public school system (Mattedi 1966, 73–8). The chairman of the party, Dr Hermes, and his successor, Jakob Kaiser, clashed with the Soviet military administration by openly objecting to the scenario it had in mind for Germany; and as a consequence, they did not last long in office before they were forced to resign (in December 1945 and December 1947 respectively).

In its appeal of 5 July 1945, the Liberal Democratic Party (LDPD) adopted a consistently negative attitude towards government inter-ference in the economy (Hohlfeld 1952; Mattedi 1966):

The takeover of private enterprises by the state is justified only when it is suitable and appropriate for the enterprise and when in the indisputable interest of the common good. This also applies to farms and estates of excessive magnitude.

But the party chairman, Dr Kunz, turned out to be a careful party strategist bent on compromise with the Soviet military administration even at the price of open tensions within the party, particularly within the Berlin branch in 1947–8. With Dr Kunz's death in April 1948, the LDPD entered a brief phase of confrontation with the SED by questioning the legitimacy of its claim on hegemony in the Soviet zone (Mattedi 1966, 142–5). In retrospect, however, this was no more than an interlude which was terminated by the removal of the acting party chairman Lieutenant and his followers from all positions of influence within the party and state apparatus pending the party congress in Eisenach on 28–9 February 1949. The congress sanctioned the return to normalcy and turned the LDPD into a minor partner of the SED.

The literature at hand, particularly the *emigré* literature, mentions numerous instances of Soviet interference in the internal affairs of the German parties,[6] which did in fact fall under the jurisdiction of the Soviet military administration by virtue of its own decree (no. 2). The purpose was that of furthering a democratic, that is socialist, development in Germany, particularly East Germany, for which the KPD and later the SED were seen as the only guarantee. In the eyes of the Soviet policy-makers in Germany, it was up to the non-communist parties and the so-called mass organizations to help the SED shoulder this responsibility; and, as a last resort, the Soviet Union was also prepared to push history in the right direction.

The pressure applied by the USSR was direct as well as indirect, discreet as well as brusque. The bourgeois party leaders reported to the Soviet military authorities on a regular basis, and stood to lose a great deal (freedom of speech, freedom of movement and other political rights) in the event of deviations from the course defined by the SED. Those who refused to give in to the warnings ran the risk of losing control of their respective parties as a result of Soviet pressure on the lower echelons of the party. The price for dissent was raised by instalments until fewer and fewer were willing to pay. In West Germany, the outcome of this process was described as a *Gleichschaltung* or streamlining of the East German non-communist parties; in East Germany, it was hailed as a victory by the progressive forces within the bourgeoisie; and in the terminology of modern political science it may be seen as a process of gradual adaptation to the *de facto* domination of the party system by the SED.[7]

This process was almost completed when two new parties emerged. The National Democratic Party (NDPD) was designed as an alternative for those who had sympathized with the war-time National Socialist Party (NSDAP) and whom the Soviet military administration wanted to reintegrate into society provided that they had not belonged to the hard core of the Nazi party. The initiative to form the party was in any event taken by a former Nazi, who wrote a letter to the editor of the *National Zeitung* (which subsequently developed into the mouthpiece of the NDPD) on the theme 'The Kind of Party I Would Like' (Mattedi 1966, 166–7), to which the national democratic circles responded so favourably that the new party was a reality within a few weeks, on 28 April 1948. Its first chairman was Dr Lothar Bolz, a Soviet citizen since 1939 and co-founder of the National Committee for a Free Germany,[8] which was intended as a political forum for German prisoners of war in the Soviet Union.

The Democratic Farmers' Party (DBD) was also a product of spontaneous initiatives in the press, in this case with *Der Freie Bauer*, serving as an intermediary. A new party was felt to be needed, since the existing parties and even the authorities did not always understand 'how to use and implement the good advice and suggestions of the occupying power'.[9] The party elected Ernst Goldenbaum, an old-time communist, to the party chairmanship, but its political ambitions were limited, as evidenced by the appeal of 25 April 1948, in which the DBD described itself in the following terms:

> Such a democratic farmers' party would not stand in any opposition to the other democratic parties, particularly not to the party of the working class. We depart from the assumption that workers and farmers are irrevocably united in the reconstruction [of Germany].

With some slight modifications, the declaration might have been issued also by the NDPD. It is not hard to imagine why the two new parties were sometimes seen as branches of the SED with the special assignment of supporting the SED against the traditional non-- communist parties; and if we are to believe Leonhard (1955), a one-time member of the ruling circles of East Berlin, such inter- pretations are not far off the mark. His source is none other than Walter Ulbricht, the East German communist party leader, who is reported to have concluded a section of a speech on communist party strategy at the Karl Marx Party School by adding that it might not be such a bad idea for the SED to get new coalition partners in the arena of party politics. But it must also be kept in mind that the new parties did have another *raison d'être*: that of mobilizing groups not attracted to an openly Marxist–Leninist platform.

*

It is hard to assign a date to the termination of the transition process in East Germany. The formal proclamation of a separate East German state on 7 October 1949 is sometimes quoted as the turning point. But by then East Germany already had all the trappings of a separate socialist state with a national-front government dominated by a Marxist–Leninist party, ministries and economic planning commissions. Yet the East Germans were not allowed to establish full-scale Soviet-style socialism. Even the name of the new republic – the German Democratic Republic (GDR) – suggested that it was somehow different from the other popular democracies. Only after the failure of the West to respond to Stalin's note of March 1952 which held out the prospect of a peace treaty with a 'unified, independent and peace-loving Germany' was Ulbricht allowed to start building full-fledged socialism. This involved the mopping up of the remnants of capitalism in East Germany – private industry (responsible for 19 per cent of production in 1952), trade (35 per cent) and the gradual collectivization of agriculture (Fowkes 1995, 26–7).

From a Marxist–Leninist point of view, the East German revolution was indeed a gift from the Soviet Union. But, for tactical reasons, the Soviet Union was reluctant to let the East German communists unravel the full implications of this gift until other scenarios for East Germany had been explored.

Czechoslovakia: Revolution with Popular Consent

It would be wrong to claim that the Soviet Union did not have anything to do with Czechoslovakia's transition to totalitarian communism. It certainly did, but at the outset at least the Soviet fist weighed less heavily on Czechoslovakia than on the other countries of Eastern Europe.

The Košice declaration of April 1945 was heavily influenced by the patriotic-front concept promoted by the Soviet Union. It vested all power in the hands of the National Front, a union of five political parties: the Communist Party of Czechoslovakia, the Czechoslovak

Social Democratic Party, the Czechoslovak National Socialist Party,[10] the Catholic People's Party and the Slovak Democratic Party. The five parties were seen as equals and were thus entitled to the same representation at all levels, except the local arena (Bankowicz 1994a, 146–7). Allegiance to the Košice programme was made into a *sine qua non* for political activity; and fascist and semi-fascist parties, including the Agrarian Party, were explicitly barred from taking part in post-war politics. This tilted the balance within the National Front in favour of the two socialist parties, the communists and the social democrats.

The post-war Czechoslovak government, nevertheless, had strongly pronounced pluralist features which carried over into the Provisional National Assembly to which the five parties in the National Front appointed 40 deputies each. And by October 1945, the allied forces, American as well as Russian, had been withdrawn from all parts of Czechoslovakia, excluding Ruthenia which was incorporated into the Soviet Union. To the extent that the Soviet Union wanted to push Czechoslovakia into Soviet-style communism, it could not simply rely on the Red Army.

*

But foreign intervention was hardly necessary at this stage. The mood of the country was distinctly leftist and the two socialist parties actually obtained a parliamentary majority of their own in the elections of May 1946. With an electoral backing of 38 per cent, the communist party emerged as the single most important party with a legitimate claim on the dominant position it already enjoyed within the National Front.

The communists had a total of 114 seats in the National Assembly. With the support of the 37 social democratic deputies, it would have been possible for communist party leader Klement Gottwald to proclaim the building of socialism right there and then. The social democrats were not stampeded into such a commitment and the communists opted for what may be described as a policy of gradual takeover. The grand coalition of five parties was retained, but with the communist party more firmly in command than before. The political platform of the new government was moderate. Prime Minister Gottwald made repeated references to 'the consolidation of nationalized industry and its coexistence with the private sector' and to a Czechoslovak 'road to socialism', different from that of the Soviet

Union (Fowkes 1995, 17). But this moderate rhetoric went hand in hand with a genuine campaign designed to smoke out actual and potential enemies of the new order from the security forces, the army, the state and local bureaucracy and to replace them by loyal communists.

By July 1947 the leaders of the National Socialist Party had drawn the conclusion that the communists were making a bid for complete hegemony in violation of the spirit of cooperation within the National Front. Apprehension was also widespread among the social democrats and within the ranks of the Slovak Democratic Party. The communists rightly saw the Slovak Democratic Party as the weakest link in an anti-communist three-partite coalition in the making and set out to neutralize it as an effective opponent. Leading Slovak politicians were brought to trial on trumped-up conspiracy charges by the communist-dominated security forces; the Slovak deputy prime minister was forced to resign and the Slovak institutions were modified so as to reduce the Slovak Democratic Party to a truly minor partner on its home turf. Such methods were later to become commonplace in the communist struggle for hegemony in post-war Czechoslovakia, but in the summer and autumn of 1947 they represented an ominous innovation (Bankowicz 1994a, 148–9).

Czechoslovakia's decision of 4 July 1947 to accept the Marshall Plan proposed by the United States, which was reversed within less than a week, is sometimes seen as the turning point in Czechoslovak politics. It was indeed a turning point in the sense that it reconfirmed the Soviet veto power in Czechoslovak foreign affairs. But in another sense the Soviet veto power was old news. Czechoslovakia's submission to Soviet foreign-policy interests had become readily apparent with the Soviet annexation of Ruthenia in 1945; and Fowkes (1995) is probably right when he suggests that the turning point did not come until September 1947 with the founding meeting of the Cominform – the communist umbrella organization replacing the Comintern. The meeting focused on the failure of the French and Italian communists to engage in a revolutionary struggle, but the Czechoslovaks – and the Hungarians – were also subject to criticism for harbouring illusions about the peaceful parliamentary road to power.

The Czechoslovak communists took this as a strong indication that they had better go on the offensive. The radicals favoured an immediate seizure of power, but this was not Gottwald's approach. In a move designed to pave the way for a communist victory in the general elections that had been called for May 1948, he opted for a strategy of stepped-up pressure on the non-communist parties and intensified purges of the security forces. Supremacy was to be gained, but in a gradual and orderly fashion, with the single list replacing the separate party lists in the upcoming elections.

This strategy might have worked had the bourgeois parties not concluded that enough was enough. The campaign against bourgeois party sympathizers within the security forces, which had been unleashed by the Ministry of the Interior, became too much for them and when Prime Minister Gottwald refused to re-examine the situation at the Ministry of the Interior, the national socialists, the Catholic People's Party and the Slovak democrats simply walked out of the government (Bankowicz 1994a, 149).

This turned out to be a fatal move. It made it possible for Gottwald to prevail upon President Beneš to accept the resignations and to fill the 12 ministerial vacancies with loyal communist supporters. This represented a deviation from standard parliamentary procedure and Beneš had promised the national socialists not to give in to that kind of pressure. But, on 25 February, after less than a week of intense courting and lobbying by Gottwald – who had mobilized the powerful communist party organization into an unprecedented show of strength – Beneš gave up his resistance and complied with Gottwald's requests (Fowkes 1995, 21–3).

The *coup d'état* of February 1948 paved the way for the elimination by the communists of the remaining vestiges of pluralism in Czechoslovakia. The single-list system was introduced in May 1948; the Social Democratic Party disappeared in June 1948 after a merger with the communists; the other non-communist parties were accepted as partners of the communist party, but only after having pledged allegiance to the leading role of the Marxist–Leninist party and after having expelled their anti-communist sympathizers.

The Guided Revolution: Poland, Hungary, Bulgaria and Romania

Unlike Hungary, Bulgaria and Romania, Poland had fought the war on the winning side. But like Hungary, Bulgaria and Romania, Poland come out of the war under the sway of the Soviet Red Army. No other country – with the possible exception of Soviet-occupied Germany – was in fact dominated by the Red Army to the same extent as Poland. Large parts of liberated Poland were actually former German territories and were for all intents and purposes treated as occupied areas by the Soviet Union even after having been turned over to the Poles (Hellén 1996; Schöpflin 1993).

Like the other three countries, Poland did not come out of the war with a strong communist movement. The Polish communists were plagued not only by organizational weakness, but by widespread distrust. The majority of the Poles correctly blamed the NKVD for the Katyn massacre and simply refused to believe that it had been the work of the German Gestapo as Stalin claimed. Though generally sympathetic to the idea of incorporating former German territories, few Poles but the communists were willing to accept the substantial territorial losses in the East imposed by the Soviet Union (Fowkes 1995, 6–7).

These circumstances made it difficult to apply the Soviet national front formula right away, and a broad national front government was not established until June 1945 after more than a year of more or less open conflict between the London-based government-in-exile on the one hand and radical local communists on the other with Moscow's Poles occupying the moderate position recommended by the Soviet authorities. This conflict coincided with peasant party leader Stanisław Mikołajczyk's return to Poland to join the Provisional Government of National Unity along with a handful of other London exiles. The broadening of the government coalition was part-and-parcel of a deal between the Soviet Union and its Western allies. Communist party leader Władysław Gomułka made it excruciatingly clear to Mikołajczyk that the communists had no intention whatsoever of giving up the position of dominance they had already acquired within the provisional government (Fowkes 1995, 10). The implication was that Mikołajczyk would have to put up a constant fight to retain his political position.

So he did, and at times with great success. Mikołajczyk's Peasant Party[11] developed into a major political force with an organizational strength surpassing that of the most favoured communists even within the urban environment (Fowkes 1995, 10). It secured a respectable 32 per cent of the votes in the 1946 referendum against the abolition of the Senate and resisted various overtures to form an electoral alliance with the communists and the social democrats in the elections that had been called for January 1947. The Polish Peasant Party made it adamantly clear that it would not be satisfied with anything short of the 50 per cent share of the parliamentary seats to which it felt entitled by virtue of Poland's distinctly rural socioeconomic profile.

This was perceived as a declaration of war by the communists, who also felt they had a legitimate claim on political hegemony; and the election campaign of 1946–7 turned into a bitter contest between the communists and their allies in the Democratic Bloc and Mikołajczyk's Polish Peasant Party. The parliamentary elections of January 1947 had all the trappings of rigged elections and produced a neat 80 per cent majority for the Democratic Bloc. With a reported electoral backing of slightly more than 10 per cent, Mikołajczyk's peasant party did come out as the strongest opposition party, but it was not enough to challenge the Democratic Bloc in the newly elected *Sejm*.

The existence of an anti-system opposition remained a source of concern for the communists. They devoted the better part of 1947 to a series of campaigns designed to wipe out and silence the opposition, though ostensibly aimed at quenching the armed anti-communist underground and at putting an end to widespread black marketeering. A number of Mikołajczyk's sympathizers were rounded up on trumped-up speculation charges; and on 20 October 1947 Mikołajczyk gave up and fled the country fearing for his life. This paved the way for the final streamlining of the Polish party system along the pattern familiar from the rest of Eastern Europe: the merger of the two socialist parties and the acceptance of those non-communist parties that agreed to serve as loyal partners of the leading Marxist–Leninist party.[12]

*

Since Béla Kun's ill-fated socialist republic of 1919, Hungary had never provided fertile ground for left-wing radicalism; and the communist party probably would not have risen to a position of prominence in post-war Hungary if it had not been for the presence of the Red Army and a Soviet-dominated Allied Control Commission. The Soviet occupation authorities were partial towards the fledgling communist movement in Hungary from the very beginning (Grzybowski 1994b, 172), but there is no evidence of direct Soviet interference in Hungarian politics until October 1945 when the Soviet chairman of the Allied Control Commission, Marshal Voroshilov, insisted that the previous grand coalition, including communists, social democrats, agrarians and liberals be continued regardless of the outcome of the upcoming general election (Fowkes 1995, 29).

So it was, and to the advantage of the communists who polled 17 per cent of the votes. This was sufficient to make the communist party the second largest party in parliament, but at a considerable distance from the winning Smallholders' Party which had an electoral backing of 57 per cent (*sic*!). It is in fact difficult to imagine a more bourgeois, and more distinctly rural, parliament than the parliament elected by the Hungarians in what was to be the last free elections in 45 years (Grzybowski 1994b, 172). It was a parliamentary setting that would normally have called for a one-party Smallholders' government with or without the support of the other parties. The communist party set out to make sure that it would never find itself in such an unfavourable situation again.

Table 3.1 Distribution of seats in the Hungarian parliament, 1945–7

Party:	Smallholders	National Peasants	Citizens' Democrats	Social Democrats	Communists
Number of seats	245	23	2	69	70
Percentage	60	6	1	17	17

Sources: Borsi (1975, 65–71); Felczak (1983, 373); Grzybowski (1994b, 174)

To that end it resorted to all the means in the unwritten manual of a revolutionary party: a policy of intimidation in collusion with the Soviet occupation authorities; the formation of a leftist bloc, including communists, social democrats and National Peasants, working within the coalition government against the allegedly reactionary policies of the Smallholders' Party; massive purges of the bureaucracy in general and the security forces in particular as well as punitive actions against the sympathizers of the old regime and outright election fraud.

The efforts paid off in the sense that the communist-dominated National Front came out as the undisputed winner of the basically rigged election of August 1947 (Grzybowski 1994b, 175). With an electoral backing of some 22 per cent and friends and allies across the political spectrum, the communist party was firmly in command, but the transition from competitive pluralism to Soviet-style totalitarianism was not yet complete.

Table 3.2 Composition of the Hungarian parliament by parties, 1947–9

	Commu-nist Party	Small-hold-ers	Social Demo-crats	Nat. Pea-sants	Total front partis	Demo-cratic People	Hung. Inde-pend.	Ind. Hung. Dem.	Others	Total oppo-sition
Seats	100	68	67	36	271	60	49	18	13	140
%	24	17	16	9	66	15	12	4	3	34

Source: Borsi (1975, 65–71); Grzybowski (1994b, 175)

The unfavourable comments about Hungary at the founding meeting of the Cominform in September 1947 helped speed up the process. By the parliamentary elections of May 1949 the communist party had absorbed the social democrats in yet another East European-style merger of the parties of the left. By that time the surviving non-communist parties had been subjected to a new wave of purges and brought into the framework of an enlarged National Front, including parties as well as officially sanctioned mass movements like the communist-dominated trade unions, youth and women's organizations, now running on a single list.

This tightly controlled and heavily supervised election produced an overwhelming majority of 95.6 per cent for the communist-dominated National Front, which hailed it as a great victory for socialism in Hungary (Révai 1949, 151–2). Four years later, shortly after the 1953 parliamentary elections, Hungary abolished the last vestiges of multi-partyism by excluding the non-communist parties from the National Front, which was retained for the purpose of running the elections and coordinating the activities of the mass organizations with those of the communist party (Grzybowski 1994b, 176).

*

Romania's and Bulgaria's road to communism was similar to that of Hungary, only much shorter and much richer in terms of overt Soviet interference. King Michael of Romania had managed to save the monarchy and large parts of the traditional political establishment by turning against Germany as the Red Army was advancing towards Romania's frontiers in August 1944. But the King was in no position to cold-shoulder the Soviet call for a broad national front-style government in Romania; and, in what seemed like a minor concession, the pitifully weak communist party obtained one ministry in the first post-armistice government. This was a modest beginning for a minor political party which was to be in complete command less than two years later; the Romanian communists clearly would not have been able to pull it off if it had not been for the relentless Soviet efforts to push history in the right direction.

By November 1944, General Vinogradov, the Soviet chairman of the Allied Control Commission, had seen to it that the influence of the National Peasant Party was curtailed to the advantage of the communist party, which obtained two additional ministries. But three ministries do not provide a solid basis for a final bid for power, particularly if they are not key ministries. By March 1946, however, the Romanian Communist Party had obtained control of three such ministries: the Ministry of the Interior, the Ministry of Justice and the Ministry of Economics. This was not enough to give the communists a majority in their own right, but, after having obtained *de facto* veto power over ministerial appointments, they did not have much cause for alarm. The Romanian communists once again owed their rapid rise to prominence to the direct intervention of their Soviet sponsors. At this particular stage, Andrei Vyshinsky, Stalin's envoy to the Balkans, made it excruciatingly clear to King Michael that he had preciously little time left to comply with the Soviet requests; and as if this were not enough, Vyshinsky's threats were accompanied by Soviet troop movements (Fowkes 1995, 34–5).

But it would probably be erroneous to attribute Romania's rapid transformation from an emerging pluralist democracy to totalitarian communism to Soviet intervention alone. Romania's ruling elites, King Michael included, had come out of the war discredited and weakened by their association and collaboration with Nazi Germany; and the underlying social tensions in this basically rural country provided ample opportunities for agitation by the communist-sponsored Ploughmen's Front (Dellenbrant 1994, 208–9). Moreover, Great Britain and the United States displayed little interest in the fate of Romania. This became abundantly clear when Great Britain and the United States went ahead and signed a formal peace treaty with Romania in February 1947 in the wake of the openly fraudulent elections of November 1946. The subsequent mop-up operations, which wiped out the monarchy as well as the multi-party format, were hardly surprising for the Western intelligence organizations covering the Balkans (Great Britain Foreign Office, Nos 374–97, 12).

*

Bulgaria's rapid transformation to totalitarian communism was also due to a combination of Soviet interference, pressure from below and British and American disinterest. But Bulgaria differed from Romania in the sense that a large section of the army was ready to cooperate with the communists. We are referring to the officers and enlisted men sympathetic to the *Zveno*, an elitist organization determined to modernize Bulgarian society from above, with ideological as well as organizational links to the Bulgarian Communist Party (Kovrig 1979, 193). The *Zveno* had joined the communist-dominated Bulgarian anti-fascist National Front as early as June 1942 and it was instrumental in thwarting the attempts by Tsar Boris to save what he could by changing his allegiance from pro-German neutrality to a neutrality favouring the anti-German alliance.

From a strictly military point of view, the allies, including the Soviet Union, were inclined to accept Tsar Boris's offer of cooperation in the war effort against Germany. From a political point of view, however, this was not sufficient to the *Zveno* and its fellow travellers within the communist-dominated National Front; the National Front therefore encouraged an uprising to make sure that it would have a decisive say in the future development of Bulgaria.

Many of the military units made common cause with the National Front and paved the way for a communist-dominated national front government, based on the parties of the left, as early as September 1944. This leftist coalition provided the communists with a badly needed platform for a final takeover (Fowkes 1995, 40–1). But it probably would not have been enough if the Soviet authorities had not embraced the cause of their Bulgarian allies and if Great Britain and the United States had not been indifferent to the fate of Bulgaria.

In November 1944, General Sergei Biryuzov, the Soviet Deputy Chairman of the Allied Control Commission, issued a decree that made it an offence for Bulgarians to communicate directly with the British and American representatives on the Allied Control Commission. When Britain and the United States failed to accept this ruling, Biryuzov simply suspended all meetings of the Allied Control Commission for three months. In January 1945 the same General Biryuzov demanded – and obtained – the resignation of a leading agrarian politician (Fowkes 1995, 41). This was in no way an isolated attempt on the part of the Soviet Union to tilt the balance in favour of the Bulgarian communists by direct interference.

It is true that the so-called percentage agreement between Churchill and Stalin had given the Western allies a 20 per cent say in Bulgarian affairs. It is also true that Great Britain and the United States made some efforts to turn the tide. But whatever they did, it was too little and too late. The protests by Russia's Western allies at best slowed down the development towards totalitarianism, but only marginally so. The elections of November 1945 and October 1946 had the trappings, but not *all* the trappings, of rigged elections. Held as they were in a climate of fraud, terror and intimidation, they produced handsome majorities for the communists and their partners within the communist-dominated Fatherland Front. There was an element of competitive pluralism, but it was eliminated as soon as it had fulfilled the purpose of paving the way for formal diplomatic recognition by Great Britain and the United States (Bankowicz 1994b, 222–9). The Bulgarian Agrarian Union (BAU) was retained as a partner of the ruling Marxist–Leninist party, but only after it had been subjugated in the all-too familiar Central and East European way.

A Comparative Analysis

The story of the communist takeover in Central and Eastern Europe is remarkably similar from country to country, but not to the point of making the countries interchangeable. With a strong and popular communist party and no foreign troops on its soil, Czechoslovakia was in fact the only country in the region to comply strictly with the Leninist model for takeover. East Germany and, for that matter, the three Baltic states – Estonia, Latvia and Lithuania – were characterized

Kaliningrad. This called for occupation and annexation (see figure 3.4). The preferred solution in Germany, however, was neutralism rather than an artificial division between two separate German states, hence Moscow's reluctance to give Ulbricht permission to start building socialism. Similar comments apply to other potential buffer states such as Czechoslovakia, Yugoslavia and Albania, where Moscow initially tried to persuade strong domestic communist parties that this was not the right time to unleash a revolution.

Poland, Hungary, Bulgaria and Romania were of much more immediate strategic concern to the Soviet Union. The three latter had been put squarely in the Soviet sphere of interest by the percentage agreement between Churchill and Stalin in October 1944 (Fowkes 1995, 28). Poland was not covered by this agreement, but – in his conversations with Churchill – Stalin made it perfectly clear that Poland must be firmly in the hands of a government promoting friendship with the USSR (Churchill 1954); from a strategic point of view, it was vital for the Soviet Union to prevent Poland from drifting away into a potential enemy camp after the far-reaching border changes involving millions of people which the Soviet Union had imposed on Poland (Hellén 1996). Poland was, therefore, to experience a rapid transition to communism under strict Soviet guidance just like Hungary, Romania and Bulgaria, the other three countries of the East European mainstream.

*

The overpowering presence of the Soviet Union had in a sense brought East European history to a halt. This was perhaps necessary in order to build Stalinism, but once Stalinism had been built and the monolithic Soviet empire was in place the suppressed political forces and processes were likely to make themselves felt with a vengeance.

Notes

1. The *de facto* incorporation of Ruthenia into the Soviet Union in November 1945 with the reluctant consent of the Czechs and the Slovaks was a minor, but highly significant, event in post-war Soviet–Czechoslovak affairs. It was an early indication of the submission of the Czechoslovak government to Soviet foreign-policy interests (cf. Bankowicz 1994a, 146–7).

2. Communism was seen as the historically inevitable outcome of the revolutionary process, but Lenin was far more interested in setting the revolutionary process in motion than in the distant millennium (cf. chapter 1).

3. With the exception of the Allied Control Commissions, Great Britain and the United States did not have any military presence at all in Eastern Europe, which was an almost exclusively Soviet domain by virtue of the Yalta and Potsdam agreements (Churchill 1954).

4. We owe this reference to Brzezinski (1965, 31).

5. As of the early 1950s, a merger with the ruling Marxist–Leninist parties was openly sought by 'progressive' elements of the Polish Democratic and United Peasant parties (Grzybowski 1994a, 48–9) and the Bulgarian Agrarian Union (Bankowicz 1994b, 228–9).

6. Leonhard (1955), with his inside reports from the *Gruppe Ulbricht,* is probably the best known.

7. For the East German version see Grosser (1963), Streisand (1980) and Schneider (1984).

8. According to Mattedi (1966, 126) and his sources, Bolz was not a member of the KPD during the Weimar period. He served as counsel for the defence in a number of trials involving communists and was disbarred in the wake of the Nazi takeover.

9. Quoted from *Der Freie Bauer* of 25 April 1948 as cited by Mattedi (1966, 130–3).

10. The National Socialist Party was a conservative, but not a fascist, political party.

11. Mikołajczyk's peasant party, also known as the Polish Peasant Party, faced competition from the left-leaning 'Wola Ludu' Peasant Party (Grzybowski 1994a, 42–3).

12. After the merger of the two peasant parties in September 1949, the Polish United Workers' Party was left as the senior partner in a three-partite coalition with the United Peasant and Democratic parties (Grzybowski 1994a, 47).

13. The term 'guided democracy' was originally coined to describe the consultative authoritarianism prevailing in some of the new democracies in the Third World of the early 1960s (Almond and Coleman 1961).

References

Almond, Gabriel A. and James Coleman (1961), *The Politics of the Developing Areas*, Princeton, Princeton University Press.

Bankowicz, Marek (1994a), 'Czechoslovakia: From Masaryk to Havel', in Sten Berglund and Jan Åke Dellenbrant, eds, *The New Democracies in Eastern Europe: Party Systems and Political Cleavages*, Aldershot, Edward Elgar.

— (1994b), 'Bulgaria; The Continuing Revolution', in Sten Berglund and Jan Åke Dellenbrant, eds, *opus cited.*

Berglund, Sten (1994), 'The Breakdown of the German Democratic Republic', in Sten Berglund and Jan Åke Dellenbrant, eds, *opus cited.*

— and Jan Åke Dellenbrant (1994), 'The Failure of Popular Democracy', in Sten Berglund and Jan Åke Dellenbrant, eds, *opus cited.*

Borsi, Emil (1975), *Az európai népi demokratikus forradalmak* (The Democratic Revolution of the Peoples of Europe), Budapest.

Brzezinski, Zbigniew K. (1965), *The Soviet Bloc: Unity and Conflict*, revised edition, New York, Frederick A. Praeger.

Churchill, Winston (1954), *The Second World War*, Vol. VI, *Triumph and Tragedy*, London.

Craig, Gordon A. (1978, 1983), *Deutsche Geschichte 1866–1945: Vom Norddeutschen Bund bis zum Ende des Dritten Reiches*, München, C. H. Beck Verlag.

Dellenbrant, Jan Åke (1994), 'Romania: The Slow Revolution', in Sten Berglund and Jan Åke Dellenbrant, eds, *opus cited*.

Felczak, Wacław (1983), *Historia Węgier* (A History of Hungary), Wrocław, Warszawa and Kraków.

Fowkes, Ben (1995), *The Rise and Fall of Communism in Eastern Europe*, 2nd edition, London, Macmillan.

Great Britain Foreign Office (1947–9), *Weekly Diplomatic Reports*, Nos 347–97, London.

Grosser, Günther (1963), 'Über die Herausbildung des Mehrparteiensystems in einigen volksdemokratischen Ländern Europas', *Zeitschrift für Geschichtswissenschaft*, Berlin, No 5.

Grzybowski, Marian (1994a), 'Poland: Towards Overdeveloped Pluralism', in Sten Berglund and Jan Åke Dellenbrant, eds, *opus cited*.

— (1994b), 'The Transition to Competitive Pluralism in Hungary', in Sten Berglund and Jan Åke Dellenbrant, eds, *opus cited*.

Hellén, Tomas (1996), *Shaking Hands with the Past: Origins of the Political Right in Central Europe*, Helsinki, The Finnish Society of Sciences and Letters and the Finnish Academy of Science and Letters.

Heym, Stefan (1974, 1990), *5 Tage im Juni*, Frankfurt am Main, Fischer Taschenbuch Verlag.

Hohlfeld, J. (1952), *Dokumente der deutschen Geschichte und Politik von 1948 bis zur Gegenwart*, vol VI, Berlin.

Kovrig, Bennett (1979), *Communism in Hungary: From Kun to Kádár*, Stanford, Hoover Institution Press.

Lenin, Vladimir I. (1905, 1963), *What Is to Be Done*, Oxford, Clarendon Press.

Leonhard, Wolfgang (1955), *Die Revolution entlässt ihre Kinder*, Ullstein, Frankfurt am Main.

Mattedi, N. (1966), *Gründung und Entwicklung der Parteien in der sowjetischen Besatzungszone Deutschlands, 1946–1949*, Bonn and Berlin, Bundesministerium für gesamtdeutsche Fragen.

Révai, József (1949), 'The Character of People's Democracy', *Foreign Affairs*, October.

Schneider, Kurt (1984), 'Zur Herausbildung und Entwicklung des sozialistischen Parteienbündnisses in der DDR unter Führung der Partei der Arbeiterklasse', *Leipziger Beiträge zur Revolutionsforschung*, No 6.

Schöpflin, George (1993), *Politics in Eastern Europe 1945–92*, Oxford, Blackwell Publishers.

Streisand, J. (1980), *Deutsche Geschichte in einem Band*, Berlin, Deutscher Verlag der Wissenschaften.

4. The Crumbling Monolith

Introduction

It is a moot question whether or not there was a blueprint for the communist takeover of Central and Eastern Europe, but there is little doubt that the outcome of the transformation process was an extremely homogeneous set of political regimes in an area previously marked by a great deal of political and economic diversity. In 1949 Czechoslovakia – the only survivor of the pre-war struggle for democracy in Central Europe and a leading industrial power in inter-war Western Europe – suddenly found itself within the same political and ideological camp as truly backward states with all but limited experiences of parliamentary democracy like the Balkan countries. Hungary and Poland had considerably less than Czechoslovakia to show by way of democratic experience, but they did have a domestic tradition of authoritarianism not entirely hostile to political pluralism, and by the end of the inter-war era the process of modernization was in full swing in both countries. Similar comments apply to the three Baltic countries – Estonia, Latvia and Lithuania – with the important proviso that they were not only integrated into the Soviet camp like the other East European countries but into the Soviet Union itself in what may be described as a belated, but successful, full-scale implementation of the Molotov–Ribbentrop Pact[1] by the victorious Red Army (Dellenbrant 1994a).

It was the Marxist–Leninist ideology with its emphasis on the time-honoured principles of the world communist movement that provided the rationale for the post-war transformation of Eastern Europe. The three most important of them may be summarized in terms of catchwords like the leading role of the communist party, democratic centralism and friendship with the Soviet Union (Berglund and Dellenbrant 1994b). Though open to various interpretations, these principles clearly left very little leeway for pluralism. The leading role of the communist party had not only have political connotations. It made the communist party into the final source of authority in all spheres of social, political and economic life. The Marxist–Leninist party had an indefinite and irreversible claim on governmental power by virtue of its self-assumed historical mission as the vanguard of the proletariat. By the same kind of rhetoric, the communist party consistently cast itself as the defender of the supposedly objective interests of the working class against the insidious subversive activities of ideological foes at home and abroad. Democratic centralism is a truly multi-dimensional concept plagued by built-in tensions between its democratic and centralistic components. It was officially argued that democracy was not possible without centralism and vice versa (Berglund and Dellenbrant 1994b), but with its emphasis on the unconditional subordination of the minority to the majority and of the lower echelons of the party hierarchy to the Central Committee and the Politburo, the Communist Party of the Soviet Union (CPSU) – and its lesser Central and East European allies – definitely put a premium on centralism rather than on democracy. The principle of friendship with the Soviet Union was officially seen as a logical extension of the Leninist notion of proletarian internationalism. It made the Soviet Union – which was the first country ever to introduce a socialist system of government – into a quasi-compulsory model for its newly found allies in Central and Eastern Europe, who duly promoted this principle to constitutional status.[2]

This ideological platform had a distinctly totalitarian streak to it. It left very little room for deviations from the Soviet model. But some deviations were in fact condoned from the very beginning. The recent converts to Soviet-style communism in Central and Eastern Europe were officially described as popular democracies,[3] and as such they were allowed to retain traces of the pre-communist structures. As noted by Otto Ville Kuusinen and his associates in their work on the foundations of Marxism–Leninism (1959), there were three phenomena that set the popular democracies apart from the Soviet Union:

1   the multi-party system;
2   the patriotic or national fronts;[4]
3   the traditional parliamentary institutions.

But in a setting marked by the leading role of the communist party and democratic centralism, the institutional differences between the Soviet

Union and the popular democracies admittedly did not add up to very much. The only non-communist parties tolerated by the regime were those that had reconciled themselves to a subordinate position in permanent alliance with the ruling Marxist–Leninist parties. Though formally broad social and political umbrella organizations, including parties, trade unions, women's and youth movements, societies for promoting friendship with the Soviet Union, etc., the patriotic or national fronts were actually dominated by communist party members.[5] In the final analysis, the parliamentary institutions were reduced to relative insignificance in a political system where elections were no longer competitive, where the parliament only convened for a few symbolic weeks every year[6] and where parliamentary dissent was almost unheard of.

*

Yet it would clearly be wrong to treat communist Central and Eastern Europe as a monolithic bloc. There were variations over time as well as among countries. In some cases the changes were initiated by the Soviet Union and/or by the local communist parties; in some cases they were not. They sometimes had profound repercussions; sometimes they did not. One of the most dramatic turning points, if not the most dramatic one, prior to the breakdown of Soviet-style communism in 1989–90, was the policy of de-Stalinization initiated by the Soviet leader Nikita Khrushchev at the twentieth party congress of the CPSU in 1956. It put an end to the most blatant cases of Soviet interference in the internal affairs of its socialist allies[7] and it introduced the notion that there might be several roads leading towards the socialist millennium.

The impact of the new Soviet policy sent shock-waves throughout the entire Soviet bloc, but nowhere with the same amplitude as in Hungary, which staged a counter-revolution that would have been successful if it had not been for Soviet military intervention. But this was not an isolated incident. The 40 years of Soviet domination in Central and Eastern Europe are in fact full of crises which testify to the inherent instability of political regimes with built-in legitimacy problems. The crises are all associated with specific years and specific countries or cities. In June 1953 the workers of East Berlin went on strike against a political regime that cut wages and stepped up production quotas in one stroke of a pen. In the autumn of 1956 the

Polish workers took similar grievances to the streets and Hungary literally exploded. In the spring of 1968, Czechoslovakia embarked on a reform programme designed to introduce 'socialism with a human face', which was brutally crushed by Soviet military intervention on 21 August.[8] In 1979–81 Poland once again found itself at the very centre of Western mass-media attention, this time on account of the spectacular success of the independent Solidarity trade union in obtaining one concession after the other from a beleaguered communist government bent on compromise.

*

Several observations may be made on the basis of this brief summary of the turbulent history of communist Central and Eastern Europe. The recurrent crises within the Soviet bloc – at the rate of at least one serious crisis every decade – were very strong indications that the Soviet model did not work. The fact that the unrest, the uprisings and the revolts had to by quenched by force – in most cases by Soviet military intervention – made this failure even more obvious (see figure 4.1). It was a limited failure, however, in the sense that it was confined to specific countries at specific points in time. Central and East European intellectuals were as a rule well informed about what was going on in neighbouring countries, but there were no snowball effects undermining the unity of the Soviet bloc until 1989–90 when Moscow openly withdrew its support from the hibernating Stalinist or neo-Stalinist regimes of Eastern Europe.

It was this Soviet hands-off policy that finally brought down the communist regimes in Bulgaria and Romania, Russia's most faithful allies in Eastern Europe from the very beginning of the communist era. The Soviet Union thus had at least two groups of allies in Central and Eastern Europe to come to grips with. On the one hand, there were the 'accident prone' countries of Central Europe – East Germany, Poland, Hungary and Czechoslovakia – which had all shaken the very foundations of the socialist system at some point in time. And, on the other hand, there were the loyalist regimes of Bulgaria and Romania which had never questioned the orthodox interpretation of principles like democratic centralism and the leading role of the Marxist–Leninist party.[9]

We believe that a systematic comparison between these two groups of countries may go some way towards accounting for the different

Figure 4.1 Protest against Soviet domination

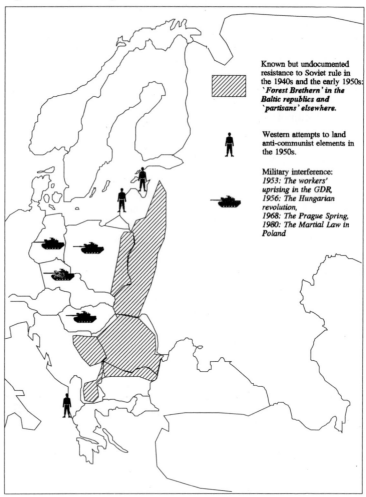

Known but undocumented resistance to Soviet rule in the 1940s and the early 1950s: *'Forest Brethern' in the Baltic republics and 'partisans' elsewhere.*

Western attempts to land anti-communist elements in the 1950s.

Military interference: *1953: The workers' uprising in the GDR, 1956: The Hungarian revolution, 1968: The Prague Spring, 1980: The Martial Law in Poland*

choices they made under communism. We also believe that a comparative analysis of the circumstances surrounding the major East European challenges to the established order – from Berlin in 1953 to Berlin and Leipzig in 1989 – may have something to tell us about the painful process of transition from totalitarianism to authoritarianism, from authoritarianism to democracy or – why not? – the other way around.

We have already seen that the ruling communist parties of Central and Eastern Europe had totalitarian ambitions from the moment they came to power until they had to give it up in 1989–90. And democracy in the Western sense of that word was not reintroduced in Central and Eastern Europe until 1989–90, at the very earliest. But this does not necessarily mean that all of Central and Eastern Europe – nor, for that matter, the Soviet Union – remained totalitarian from the beginning of the cold war until the demise of the communist system of government in the late 1980s and early 1990s. It is, therefore, only appropriate that we continue our investigation with a section on the difficult art of classifying communist regimes. In the two following sections we will return to the question of what makes for stable versus unstable communist totalitarianism with the benefit of the hindsight provided by the *débâcle* of 1989–90.[10]

The Difficult Art of Classifying Communist Regimes

The communist regimes of Central and Eastern Europe officially portrayed themselves as democracies. The rules of the game that were imposed by the governing Marxist–Leninist parties not only precluded free and fair elections but open competition for political power among rival political elites, and the ambitions of the ruling communist parties were indeed *totalitarian* throughout the entire communist era.[11] But it is an open question to what extent the communist parties succeeded in creating the totalitarian society they wanted; and to the extent that they did not, it would perhaps be more accurate to describe the regime as *authoritarian*.

This is not just a conceptual subtlety. We use the terms totalitarianism and authoritarianism in a manner that is consistent with that of Friedrich and Brzezinski (1965) and Linz (1964, 1974). The totalitarian regime sets out to control *all* aspects of social life, while the authoritarian regime attempts to accommodate and co-opt certain conflicting interests in order to preserve the power and authority of the ruling elite. While pluralism is anathema to the practitioners of totalitarianism, it is a fact of life for authoritarian rulers. Nazi Germany (1933–45) and the Soviet Union of the 1930s and 1940s are clear-cut cases of totalitarianism. Central and Eastern Europe also qualify as totalitarian, at least prior to Stalin's death in 1953 and probably until the twentieth congress of the CPSU. But what about the aftermath? Was there a point in time when the communist parties tacitly gave up their totalitarian ambitions and started operating according to the precept of the authoritarian power broker anxious to preserve his privileged position? We believe there was such a point in time in the history of most of the Central European countries, and perhaps even in the history of the Balkan countries. We also have reason to believe that the process was gradual and piecemeal and, therefore, difficult to pinpoint.

A modern society is a complex society. It is a society with a high degree of structural differentiation and specialization and is profoundly marked by cultural secularization. It is more difficult to control and manipulate than less-developed, more primitive societies. Huntington and Brzezinski (1965) therefore assumed that the programme of rapid modernization – to which the leaders of the Soviet Union and their allies in Eastern Europe were deeply committed – would be conducive to pluralism in the long run.[12] This was indeed the case, but it was pluralism of the guided and closely monitored variety. As will be argued at some length further on, politics does matter, and the Soviet leaders and their East European allies had no intention whatsoever of letting the situation get out of hand. But even dictators do not always have their way. Like all politicians, they operate under a variety of domestic and external constraints, and it is probably fair to say that the Soviet and East European leaders became more and more dependent on the major institutional interest groups as time went by. It was in a sense a slightly more sophisticated version of the in-fighting between heavy and light industry, between industry and farming and between plan and market within the Soviet Communist Party in the 1930s (Parland 1993), but it was only slightly more sophisticated. The stakes remained high for the individual participants in this oblique and convoluted political debate, where a recklessly worded argument might be construed as an attack on the leading role of the Marxist–Leninist party and on the principle of democratic centralism.[13]

Neo-Stalinism – the slightly liberalized version of Stalinism that was introduced after Stalin's death in March 1953 – did have some authoritarian features, but it would seem natural to require more from an authoritarian society than a certain amount of political pluralism and inter-elite competition. Juan Linz certainly does in his seminal article on Spain under Franco (1964), where, among other things, he makes a point of the predictability of the way in which an authoritarian regime actually exercises its formally ill-defined power.[14] The authoritarian ruler cannot operate as an efficient power broker unless individual citizens feel free to articulate their needs, wishes and interests; and individual citizens presumably would not feel free to do so unless they enjoyed a certain amount of legal, social and moral support.

Concepts like rule of law and civil society spring to mind. These are attributes of democratic societies, but not only of democratic societies (Sartori 1965, 1987). The constitutional monarchies of Northern and Central Europe prior to the First World War, including the Wilhelmine and Austro-Hungarian empires, qualify on both counts. They were not absolute, but constitutional monarchies and they did have a civic culture conducive to interest-articulation and citizen participation (Aarebrot and Berglund 1995). By the end of the 1980s preciously few of the East European countries qualified, but at least two of them had nevertheless moved considerably towards rule of law and civil society.

We are referring to Poland and Hungary. Poland – which had entered the post-war era as a Soviet fiefdom – gradually edged out of the Soviet iron fist and developed into somewhat of a hotbed of East European political dissent. The Polish road to socialism, as proclaimed by Władysław Gomułka upon his political rehabilitation and return to power, in the wake of the twentieth party congress of the Communist Party of the Soviet Union,[15] displayed uniquely Polish features such as a reversal of the commitment to collectivization and a belated recognition of the importance of the Catholic church. In an ironical twist of history, Gomułka – who had been called back from his involuntary political exile as a result of the strikes and political unrest in Poznań in the summer of 1956 – was ousted from the office of first party secretary shortly before Christmas 1970 in the face of widespread unrest among the workers. This had been brought about by new radical increases in the prices of food and fuel introduced by the government. After a brief spell of success on borrowed money with unprecedented growth rates, Edward Gierek, the new party secretary, ran into the same kinds of problems as his predecessor and found himself replaced by Stanisław Kania, a middle-of-the-road party bureaucrat whose efforts to change the course of events were to no avail.

If anything, the situation took a turn for the worse. By the late 1970s, economic realities called for massive contraction and cutbacks; the workers came out in uncompromising defence of their economic and political rights and set out to form coalitions with the intellectual segments of the anti-system opposition along a pattern familiar from 1956 (Brzezinski 1965, 250–5).

These were the formative years of Solidarity, the first officially recognized independent trade union in the Soviet bloc. But Solidarity was not just a trade union. It served as a rallying point and an umbrella organization for most of the dissident groups in Poland and it did not hesitate to promote political demands along with traditional unionist bread-and-butter issues such as the 40-hour work week and the call for a price freeze. Western-style parliamentary democracy was held out as the ultimate objective by some groups within this heterogeneous organization, most notably by the Workers' Defence Committee (KOR). The government used this kind of anti-system dissent as an excuse for clamping down on the opposition, but the imposition of martial law on 13 December 1981 by General Wojciech Jaruzelski, Kania's successor as first secretary of the United Workers' Party, was also designed to deprive the Soviet Union of a pretext for yet another military intervention of the kind that had crushed the Prague Spring of 1968.

Martial law did keep the Soviet troops at arm's length and it did buy the beleaguered regime precious time. All Solidarity activities were suspended; the top-level Solidarity leaders, including Lech Wałęsa, the legendary trade-union activist, who had brought the Gierek regime to the negotiating table in 1979, were detained in prison camps on Poland's border with the Soviet Union; censorship was reintroduced and Poland was virtually cut off from the rest of the world. This dealt a severe blow to Solidarity, but it was not enough to bring the organization into complete disarray.

By the time the regime lashed out against the opposition, Solidarity had already made an indelible imprint on the Polish political system as an independent partner in the decision-making process. Within a few short months of its official recognition by the communist regime in the summer of 1979, it had recruited some 9.5 million dues-paying members in a country with approximately 40 million inhabitants.[16] Some 40 000 activists had been promoted to regular staff positions. A National Coordinating Committee had been formed in Gdańsk under the leadership of Lech Wałęsa: and the National Coordinating Committee was constantly in touch with the regional and local committees through a system of telephone and telex links. This kind of social network does not disappear overnight with the imposition of martial law. It goes underground; and, though weakened, Solidarity remained a formidable threat to the communist regime almost from the very beginning of martial law.

The attempts by the regime to undermine and render Solidarity superfluous by creating alternative structures of social inclusion such as the Patriotic Movement for National Rebirth (PRON) in the aftermath of martial law met with little success. The regime finally gave in to the pressure from Solidarity, the Catholic church, foreign governments and human-rights groups abroad and initiated the 1986 amnesty. This marked the beginning of the tortuous process that was to lead up to the round-table negotiations between the communist regime and the anti-system opposition in the spring of 1989 and the first free or almost free parliamentary elections in more than 40 years on 4 June 1989. The communist regime was by no means ideologically committed to dialogue and compromise with the opposition, but Solidarity literally forced the regime into negotiations by making it excruciatingly clear that the political and economic crisis in Poland could not be solved without the active participation of Solidarity. The successful boycott of the November 1987 referendum on the state of the economy[17] and the strike wave of 1988 in the face of new price hikes had sent a loud and clear message to the government (Jenkins 1992).

The pledge to free or almost free elections in the round-table negotiations was a major concession on the part of the government. But it was not tantamount to unconditional surrender. In return for its formal recognition and re-legalization on 17 April 1989, Solidarity had to agree to a power-sharing arrangement with the ruling United Workers' Party and its two long-standing allies, the Democratic and the United Peasant parties. The latter were to receive no less than 65 per cent of the seats in the *Sejm* in what basically amounted to uncontested elections. Solidarity was free to run for the remaining 35 per cent of the seats in the *Sejm* and all the 100 seats in the newly created Upper House, the Senate.

The election nevertheless turned into a resounding victory for Solidarity. It conquered just about all the contested seats[18] and in the process it humiliated the governing coalition severely. Several of the candidates for the governing coalition, who ran unopposed, did not receive the 50 per cent of votes required to be elected and therefore could not stand in the second round of the elections (Jenkins 1992). But it was not the poor election results that brought the communist regime down. It was the post-electoral coalition between Solidarity on the one hand and the Democratic and United Peasant parties on the other hand that paved the way for a government under the leadership of Solidarity activist Tadeusz Mazowiecki, Poland's first non-communist prime minister since the late 1940s (Grzybowski 1994a). Technically speaking, the Mazowiecki government was a four-party coalition, including the United Workers' Party, which retained control of sensitive ministries such as Defence, the Interior and Communications, and formally the four-party coalition rallied behind Wojciech Jaruzelski for president. But for the United Workers' Party and General Jaruzelski, the architect of martial law and, for Polish popular democracy, this was the beginning of the end.

*

The Hungarian road to democracy followed a different path. It was strongly marked by the traumatic events of the November uprising in 1956, when Soviet troops put an end to the short-lived Hungarian experiment in democracy by the local communist regime. Long before the proclamation under similar circumstances of the so-called Brezhnev doctrine in 1968, the Soviet intervention in Hungary in 1956 sent a loud and clear message to the rest of the world – and particularly to Moscow's allies – that there was a definite limit to the amount of diversity that the Soviet Union was willing to tolerate within its own camp. Parliamentary democracy and military neutrality – to which the Hungarian Communist Party under Imre Nagy had pledged itself under the impact of popular demands – could not be reconciled with the principles of Marxism–Leninism as understood by Moscow. But the intervention also had a price tag attached to it for the Soviet Union, the World Communist Movement and last, but not least, for the Hungarian communists (Grzybowski 1994b).

The regime which was installed by Moscow in the wake of the so-called counter-revolution had all the attributes of a puppet regime. It clearly did not have the mandate of the people. It had responded to a call from the Soviet Union, and in spite of his credentials as a one-time communist dissident, János Kádár, Moscow's choice for prime minister, was generally perceived as a traitor after having turned his back on the Nagy regime during the critical days prior to the Soviet military intervention.[19] Of all the communist regimes at the time, the Kádár regime probably had the thinnest possible basis of legitimacy.

In the short run, there was little Kádár could do to improve his image at home and abroad. The first few years after the uprising were marked by political repression and enforced agricultural collectivization, while Kádár set out to create a platform for himself and his followers of young activists and technocrats (Nowak 1984, 34). The old Hungarian Workers' Party was transformed into a new Hungarian Socialist Workers' Party (HSWP) entirely dominated by supporters of the new regime. A great deal of attention was devoted to promoting good relations with the Soviet Union, and in the long run Kádár was even seen as the architect of a *modus vivendi* with the Soviet Union based on mutual respect and loyalty (Gati 1986, 206). The understanding with the Soviet Union was particularly important, since the regime opted for a policy of political as well as economic reform after the initial phase of repression (Hellén 1996).

The reforms were piecemeal, gradual and somewhat erratic. The overall thrust was towards pluralism, but with the overriding proviso that it must not jeopardize the leading role of the Marxist–Leninist party. The one-party format – which had been introduced in 1953 – was not abandoned, but an element of competition among the candidates running for election was introduced in 1967 and in 1983 multi-candidate elections became mandatory. The rule of law was strengthened through the introduction of pseudo-independent institutions for the purpose of monitoring compliance with the constitution by the authorities, and a variety of economic reforms were introduced.

The Hungarian economic reform process – which was to inspire Yuri Andropov and Mikhail Gorbachev to proclaim *perestroika* in the Soviet Union years later – was in fact initiated in the early 1960s and by 1968 the new policy had become known as the New Economic Mechanism (NEM). It called for the scrapping of central planning with compulsory targets in every sphere of economic life, for decentralized decision-making and for a careful experiment in market prices. The reform process was long-winded and not without setbacks (Jenkins 1992, 123), but in the long run it helped bring about a sizeable private sector in Hungary. The growth of this sector was in a sense a byproduct of a spontaneous movement by people interested in improving their material conditions by 'exploiting themselves'. In the late 1970s, two thirds of Hungarian households reported earning additional money from what was referred to as the 'second sector', mainly by providing agricultural products and various services on the market (Deppe and Hoss 1989, 40), by the 1980s the 'second sector' had infiltrated the very core of the Hungarian economy:

> For ideological reasons, it was not a path the government and the party were happy to take, and even less, compared to Gierek's Poland, a conscious exploitation of populism. But with the Kádárist system hinging so much on delivering decent material conditions, the step-by-step privatisation of ever larger sectors of the economy had to be tolerated (Hellén 1996).

The growth of a second, independent, sector, with all the social networks and organizations that entailed, did pose a threat to the power monopoly cherished by the Hungarian Socialist Workers' Party, but the anti-system opposition long remained a marginal phenomenon. It hardly reached beyond the symbolic activities of scattered intellectuals until the mid-1980s, when it rapidly developed into somewhat of a mass movement. This rapid transformation of the political landscape would not have been possible if it had not been encouraged by reform-minded top-level Hungarian communists like Imre Pozsgay, a member of the Central Committee and the leader of the Hungarian Patriotic Front. In an unorthodox move for a bearer of a Marxist–Leninist heritage, Pozsgay even attended the founding meeting in 1987 of the Hungarian Democratic Forum (HDF), which was to become one of the major Hungarian opposition parties of conservative vintage in the struggle for parliamentary democracy. Two liberal parties, the Alliance of Free Democrats and FIDESZ, followed suit and by the end of 1988 and the beginning of 1989 the parties familiar from the inter-war era, the Smallholders, the Social Democrats and the Christian Democrats, had begun to reorganize in order to run in the parliamentary elections scheduled for January 1990 by the parties to the roundtable.

The changes within the ruling Hungarian Socialist Workers' Party were no less dramatic. The hard-liners, with whom the ageing and ailing Kádár had aligned himself, made a last-ditch attempt to turn the clocks backwards at the party congress in May 1988, but to no avail. The Kádárists were literally swept out of the Politburo, but the tensions between hard-liners like Károly Grósz and reformists such as Imre Poszgay carried over into the reformed party, which split down the middle in the aftermath of the extraordinary party congress in October 1989. The government remained in the hands of the hard-liners, who reconstituted the party under the old party label, but it had little choice but to continue the dialogue with the opposition. The dialogue was not without complications,[20] but as in Poland it eventually resulted in roundtable negotiations between government and opposition that provided a platform for a peaceful transition from communism at the polls. But unlike their Polish comrades, the Hungarian communists did not make any provisions for a soft landing in the form of uncontested, safe seats. The democratic breakthrough was complete; and the parliamentary elections – the first round of which were held in January 1990 – were indeed free elections.

*

The differences between Polish and Hungarian roads to parliamentary democracy should not make us oblivious of the many similarities. The transition processes were regime initiated in more ways than one. In Hungary the regime initially promoted political opposition only to give in to it, when the opposition was gaining the upper hand. In Poland the regime finally caved in under the pressure of a political opposition which had been building up strength over at least the two past decades. In Poland the regime provided a platform for dissent by opting for a *modus vivendi* rather than all-out conflict with the powerful Catholic church, by reneging on its pledge to collectivize the agricultural sector and by tolerating and even promoting a small, but thriving, private sector. In Hungary the careful and continuous process of privatization extending into the very core of industrial production under the banner of the New Economic Mechanism paved the way for a web of independent or semi-independent social networks and organizations more or less beyond government control.

By the mid-1980s, these two countries were a far cry from the blind and arbitrary totalitarianism of the early 1950s. The communist rulers of Poland and Hungary were admittedly reluctant to give up their claim on power monopoly, the former probably more so than the latter, but by the mid-1980s they were, nevertheless, no strangers to dialogue and even negotiations with the opposition. In the process, the rule of law was strengthened as was the participant kind of civic culture. Even by our stringent criteria, there is thus a good case to be made for classifying the communist regimes of Poland and Hungary as *authoritarian* rather than totalitarian several years before the formal breakdown of communism in 1989–90. In this respect, Poland and Hungary were exceptional in the East European context.

*

East Germany was also exceptional, but only due to the provisional character of the East German state. The existence of a separate East German state was never fully accepted by West Germany, not even in the spirit of *détente* and mutual cooperation between the two German states of the early 1970s. Nor did the East Germans reconcile themselves with the arbitrary partitioning of the country into watertight compartments between East and West during the cold war between the former allies of the anti–Hitler coalition. Millions of East Germans fled to West Germany before the border was fortified and the Berlin wall came up in August 1961. This drastic move reduced the exodus to a trickle. It probably saved the battered East German economy from imminent collapse, but it did little to enhance the prestige of the beleaguered communist regime at home and abroad. As if this were not enough, it was readily apparent that the communist regime was entirely dependent on the Soviet Union.

It was a dependence that surpassed that of Moscow's other allies in Central and Eastern Europe. East Germany had been 'liberated' from fascism by the 'victorious and glorious Soviet Red Army' which promoted the interests of the communist party and its allies. The same Red Army was called upon to put down the first serious challenge against the communist system, when in June 1953 the workers of East Berlin went on strike against a workers' and farmers' state that had the cheek to cut salaries and increase production quotas with one stroke of the pen. But the Soviet Union was far from an unconditional ally of its East German brethren and was no stranger to playing out its German card in its negotiations with the West. The prospect of German reunification with all its ominous ramifications for the East German regime and for the former German territories under Polish and Soviet administration was long held out as a potential reward for West German neutrality as opposed to the close cooperation with the Western powers preferred by the conservative Adenauer regime (1949–63). Adenauer advocated negotiations with the Soviet Union, but only from a position of strength provided by a clear-cut commitment to NATO and its allies.

It goes without saying that the climate of confrontation between West Germany and East Germany, compounded as it was by the fear that the Soviet Union would somehow renege on its ideological commitment towards the communist regime in East Germany, did not create an ideal situation for whatever organized anti-system opposition there was in the German Democratic Republic, and the truth of the matter is that there were preciously few such groups. There was the standard set of East European protest groups like pacifists, peace activists and scattered human-rights groups of a religious (especially Evangelical and Lutheran) flavour,[21] but, as a rule, these groups kept a low profile throughout the 1970s and 1980s. The counter-strategies of the regime covered the whole range from infiltration – the full extent of which did not become apparent until the files of the dreaded Ministry for State Security had fallen into the hands of the opposition in the wake of the peaceful revolution of 1989 – and repression, including the broadly publicized practice of putting individual system critics on one-way trips to West Berlin – a somewhat ambiguous punishment in a country with closed borders – to outright adaptation to the prevailing mood of the country. The SED approach to disarmament in 1984, which was to become a year of unprecedented armament on both sides of the Iron Curtain, is a case in point. It testifies to a strategy of appeasement towards West Germany and adaptation to the widespread anti-war feelings at home. The military build-up by the Warsaw Pact countries, particularly by the GDR, is portrayed as a necessary and unfortunate counter-measure at a time when American Pershing II and cruise missiles were being deployed in Western Europe, particularly in the Federal Republic of Germany, and *not* as a contribution to the European system of security (*Neues Deutschland*, 31 December 1984).

On the whole, however, the communist rulers of East Germany did *not* opt for accommodation and dialogue with the low-keyed anti-system opposition. The communist regime launched a largely successful programme designed to improve the material lot of the East Germans which made the East German economy into a showcase planned economy, but *hélas* with a performance rate not on a par with that of the flourishing market economy in neighbouring West Germany, and it embarked on a less than successful campaign designed to promote a separate East German national identity (Berglund 1994).

The extent of the legitimacy deficit became obvious in the spring, summer and autumn of 1989, when East Germans were once again given an opportunity to 'vote with their feet' and emigrate to West Germany, at this juncture by way of neighbouring Hungary and Poland which were already on their way out of the socialist camp and had little interest in preventing East German tourists from proceeding to

West Germany.[22]   When this escape route was cut off by the desperate Honecker regime, thousands of East Germans headed for Czecho-slovakia – one of the few countries for which an East German exit visa was not required – where they sought refuge on the West German embassy compound. This was a source of major embarrassment to the communist regime in East Germany, where the stage was being set for a solemn celebration on 7 October 1989 commemorating the foundation of the German Democratic Republic 40 years earlier in the presence of a number of foreign dignitaries, including Soviet party leader Mikhail Gorbachev. East Berlin was anxious to remove the Prague refugees from the agenda and granted them free passage to West Germany, but only on condition that they be transitted to West Germany by way of East Germany. This decision turned out to be a fatal mistake. The train carrying the refugees was met by demonstrations and riots at every stop on its journey through East Germany. The demonstrations were directed, *not* against those who were allowed to leave, but against a regime that restricted the freedom to travel, and provided additional fuel to the popular unrest that had swept through the major cities of East Germany, particularly Leipzig, Berlin and Dresden, since May 1989.

As if this were not enough, Gorbachev – who had long been at odds with the hibernating Stalinist and neo–Stalinist regimes in Eastern Europe – used the fortieth anniversary of the GDR to warn Erich Honecker publicly that leaders who failed to respond to popular pressures 'put themselves in danger' (East 1992). Less than two weeks later Honecker had resigned and been replaced by Egon Krenz, Honecker's heir apparent who now pledged himself to political reform. Krenz's democratic credential were less than convincing and he found himself removed from office and replaced by Hans Modrow, the reform-minded SED leader of Dresden, within less than two months. This marked the beginning of genuine pluralism, dialogue and round-table negotiations between government and opposition which paved the way for the first and last free parliamentary elections in the short history of the GDR on 18 March 1990. But by then the agenda had changed fundamentally. What had started out as a call for democratic reform within the framework of the existing state structure had turned into a massive movement for German unification. It was a development for which the regime and the anti-system opposition – which retained a distinct socialist flavour – were poorly prepared, but it was actively and successfully promoted by the East German

Christian Democrats who had severed their ties with the SED and aligned themselves with the ruling Christian Democrats of the Federal Republic.

*

Czechoslovakia was exceptional in yet another sense. It was the only East European country to enter the post-war era with solid pre-war democratic credentials and an uncontestable record as an advanced industrial nation, and yet it ended up with one of the most repressive Stalinist regimes after the *coup d'état* staged by the Czechoslovak communists in February 1948. The Stalinist excesses of the Gottwald regime (1948–53) with its show trials, purges and political executions, carried over into the post-Stalinist era, albeit on a more subtle scale, and provided fertile ground for Alexander Dubček's reform movement of the late 1960s. Dubček, who had been elected party secretary in February 1968, set out to provide 'socialism with a human face' by encouraging an open debate and relaxing a number of the restrictions imposed by his predecessors, including censorship and the ban on factions. Society responded quickly to the new cues. The once-silent partners of the communist party in the National Front were revitalized; parties once banned started to reorganize and by the summer of 1968 the old, pre-1948 party system, had basically re-emerged.

As seen from Moscow's perspective, all this was very bad news indeed. It was reminiscent of the Hungarian counter-revolution back in 1956. The leading role of the communist party was being eroded; democratic centralism was not being upheld and there was widespread, but probably unfounded, fear in Moscow that the new leaders in Czechoslovakia would renege on their commitment to the Warsaw Pact.[23] In the final analysis, the failure of the Czechoslovak government to comply with the 'friendly suggestions' from Moscow and its four faithful allies within the Warsaw Pact left Moscow with two alternatives, both of them rather unpleasant: to let the Czechs and the Slovaks build socialism as they saw fit with the possible snowball effects which that might entail within the Soviet bloc or to impose the Soviet model by force and face international condemnation and isolation.

The invasion of Czechoslovakia by Soviet, Bulgarian, East German, Hungarian and Polish troops[24] in the night of 20–21 August 1968 made it adamantly clear that there were still very definite limits to the kind of diversity that could be tolerated within the Soviet bloc. It was a successful military operation which met only with passive resistance and resulted in a return to Soviet-style orthodoxy or 'normalization'. The Marxist–Leninist party reasserted its monopoly of power within all spheres of social, political and economic life. Dissent was brutally repressed and no less than 320 000 of the party members (21 per cent of the total) were purged from the party in the aftermath of the Soviet invasion.

There were to be only minor deviations from this orthodox party line over the next 20 years, and then only under the impact of the Soviet policies of *glasnost* and *perestroika* promoted by Mikhail Gorbachev (Jenkins 1992, 134); and with Gustáv Husák as president, Ladislav Adamec as prime minister and Miloš Jakeš as leader of the communist party, the hard-liners seemed to have things pretty much under control almost until the bitter end in November 1989. They remained unchallenged within the party, and to the extent that there was a dialogue with the small, but vocal, dissident groups like Charter 77, it occurred in the courtrooms and not in parliament, nor at round- table negotiations (Jenkins 1992, 134–35).

It was the successful revolt of the East German masses in late October and early November 1989 that inspired the peoples of Czechoslovakia to political action and brought new life into the existing anti-system networks which rallied under the banner of the *Civic Forum* (in the Czech Republic) and *Public against Violence* (in the Slovak Republic). This marked the beginning of a short, intensive dialogue between government and opposition which resulted in the unconditional surrender of the communist regime to the democratic forces within less than a month. By then, the communist party had given up its claim on power monopoly and the old guard, including President Gustáv Husák, had left the stage after having handed over power to men and women who had been standing trial for subversive activities a few months or weeks earlier. The dual choice of Václav Havel for president and Alexander Dubček for speaker of the national assembly testifies to the complete rejection of Marxism–Leninism as understood by Moscow's middle-men in Czechoslovakia ever since the late 1960s. The former was a renowned poet and long-time dissident, constantly harassed by the security police, and the latter the chief architect of the Prague Spring of 1968 and as such Czechoslovakia's most famous non-person until November 1989.

The breakdown of communism in Czechoslovakia thus cannot be attributed to the existence of a strong anti-system opposition movement as in Poland and, to some extent, in Hungary. In Czechoslovakia – and in East Germany – initially small and weak anti-system opposition groups gained strength and impetus from widespread popular discontent and unrest. The discontent had built up over decades of political oppression, alleviated only by acceptable economic performance rates, and was bound to come into the open as soon as it was reasonably safe to articulate political grievances. When he openly castigated the Honecker regime for not being more responsive to the people, Mikhail Gorbachev indirectly opened up the floodgates of political change in East Germany. And once they felt reassured that the Soviet Union was *not* planning a rerun of the dramatic and traumatic events of 1968, the Czechs and the Slovaks followed suit. In both cases, however, the breakdown of communism was a byproduct of an underlying legitimacy crisis, by no means unique to East Germany and Czechoslovakia but perhaps more acutely felt in East Germany and Czechoslovakia than in Poland and Hungary by virtue of the intransigent approach to opposition adopted by the East German and Czechoslovak communist regimes.

*

Moscow's most faithful allies in Eastern Europe – Bulgaria and Romania – hardly earned any reputation for political dissent until the very eve of the *débâcle* in 1989–90. There were times, when the underlying tensions within the ruling communist parties came into the open[25], but Bulgaria and Romania actually did not have an organized anti-system movement comparable even to the low-keyed East German and Czechoslovak peace and human-rights groups.

It is tempting to blame the absence of opposition on the political climate of fear and repression cultivated by the omnipotent Bulgarian and Romanian security forces. There is indeed a good case to be made for the notion that Bulgaria and Romania perhaps had the *most* repressive totalitarian regimes in the history of communist Eastern Europe.[26] But we believe there is more to it than that. We are, after all, talking about countries with a common past in the Ottoman empire with all that entails by way of feudal traditions. In his highly informative exposé of the recent revolutions in Eastern Europe, Roger East

(1992) describes Todor Zhivkov's Bulgaria (1961–89) in the following way.

> [Zhivkov's] power was exercised through a regional and local network of party barons, on an almost feudal model. It was, in consequence, an inherently conservative structure, with power at all levels in the hands of a 'mafia' whose primary impulses were concerned with retaining their status and advantages.

Ceauşescu's Romania (1965–89) and his contemporary heirs are frequently analysed in similar terms. Referring to the pervasive legacy of corruption, Trond Gilberg (1992, 296–7) concludes that there is a 'real danger that corruption will continue [and] that new bosses will behave in old ways'. The literature at hand is also full of references to Ceauşescu's sultanistic habit of treating his country as a personal fiefdom to be controlled by a closed network of relatives and family friends (East 1992, 138). In a historical perspective, these are admittedly authoritarian rather than totalitarian practices, but in these particular cases they clearly worked in favour of party leaders with absolute or totalitarian ambitions.

It was probably to the advantage of Todor Zhivkov and his predecessors to operate in an environment where Russians have tended to be perceived as liberators rather than oppressors ever since the breakdown of the Ottoman empire. In Romania, the strange combination of Stalinism at home and an increasingly independent foreign policy that characterized the entire Ceauşescu era, probably benefitted the regime in a number of ways. It added to the international prestige of the regime and made Nicolae Ceauşescu into a most favoured East European middle-man in international politics. It contributed significantly to Romania's credit-rating on the Western money markets and, for a while at least, it probably helped defuse whatever might have been left of protest potential on the tightly controlled domestic stage.

This list of underlying causes does not purport to be exhaustive. But we would argue that it is sufficient to account for the rather slow and belated reactions in Bulgaria and Romania to the dramatic changes that were taking place throughout Eastern Europe in the summer and autumn of 1989. Among the latecomers to the democratic transition, Bulgaria was the first one out, followed by Romania. This left Albania

– a truly deviant case in the East European context – as the last hibernating Stalinist regime by the early 1990s.[27]

In Bulgaria, the breakdown of the communist regime was initiated from within and came in the form of a palace coup, staged by foreign minister Peter Mladenov on 9 November 1989 in order to avert the mounting criticism of the Zhivkov regime for its high-handed approach towards the small, but vocal, Bulgarian environmentalist movement which went to great lengths to have Bulgaria put on the agenda of the ongoing CSCE conference on environmental affairs (Bankowicz 1994b). This marked the beginning of a rapid reform process which paved the way for free elections in June 1990. With the exception of the Albanian elections in 1991, these were the only East European founding elections formally won by a reformed communist party, the Bulgarian Socialist Party (BSP). The weakness of the opposition which had but a few months to organize and prepare for the elections goes a long way towards accounting for this outcome, but the electoral victory of the socialist party was also a tribute to the strength of the feudal or semi-feudal networks on which the communist regime had relied.

In Romania, the regime refused to give in to the mounting discontent that it had brought upon itself by embarking on urbanization and austerity programmes of unparalleled severity, even for Eastern Europe (Dellenbrant 1994b), and it was literally overthrown by force in what amounted to a bloody civil war between loyalist *Securitate* forces on the one hand and rebellious army units on the other. In the official rhetoric of the victorious rebels, the army was portrayed as responding to a call from the people, but the chain of events would seem to suggest that Ion Iliescu and his followers had been planning a palace coup against his mentor, Nicolae Ceauşescu, long before the regime was destabilized by popular unrest before Christmas 1989. The fact that the National Salvation Front (NSF) of Ion Iliescu took over almost the entire apparatus of the outlawed communist party also testifies to the strong element of continuity in post-war Romanian politics (Dellenbrant 1994b). The resounding electoral victory of the National Salvation Front in the elections which were held in May 1990 should thus at least partly be attributed to the resilience of the semi-feudal organizational networks forged by the Ceauşescu regime.

*

Of the six countries or political systems covered at length in this section, there are only two clear-cut cases of authoritarianism – Poland and Hungary – and then only towards the latter part of the 1980s. The uprising by the workers of East Berlin in June 1953 was a source of embarrassment to the Soviet Union and its allies in the newly founded German Democratic Republic, but it did not constitute a serious threat to the Soviet system of government. The Prague Spring of 1968 represented such a challenge. It was an attempt by the Czechoslovak communists to promote genuine as opposed to formal pluralism, to reintroduce the rule of law and to turn subjects into citizens. But it was thwarted by Soviet military intervention which brought Czechoslovakia back into the Soviet fold where it was to remain along with Bulgaria, East Germany and Romania until the breakdown of communism in 1989–90.

By the 1980s, the communist parties of these four countries had the revolutionary stage way behind them. What had started out as a grand scheme for social transformation with the Marxist–Leninist party in the driver's seat had turned into a tedious and cumbersome administrative project with the communist party desperately trying to hold on to the steering wheel.[28]   In the process, the ruling communist parties admittedly resorted to a variety of authoritarian devices familiar from a feudal, nationalistic and even religious past, but the regimes nevertheless remained totalitarian. The ambitions of the ruling communist parties were definitely totalitarian from the introduction of popular democracy to its demise; and, though not entirely immune to change, Bulgaria, Czechoslovakia, East Germany and Romania had preciously little by way of genuine pluralism, rule of law or civic culture on the eve of the *débâcle* in 1989–90.

Dictatorships Tend to Be Poor

Economic development is frequently cast as a necessary, if not even a sufficient, prerequisite for democracy. This is in fact one of the underlying notions of the so-called convergence theories. The more developed Russia or the Soviet Union would become, the more it would acquire by way of structural differentiation and cultural secularization and the more difficult it would become to run the country by Stalinist methods (cf. Almond and Powell 1978). Non–Stalinist methods are not necessarily democratic methods, but it was correctly assumed that deviations from the Stalinist model would bring the country closer to the US or West European mainstream (Huntington 1968).

Table 4.1 Socioeconomic indicators for Central and Eastern Europe

		Poland	CSSR	Hung.	GDR	Bulgar.	Roman.	Alban.	FRG	Highest	
Urban population, %	1950	23	14	38	20	9	10	0	48	71	(UK)
(in cities 100000+)	1960	27	14	22	21	14	16	8	51	72	(UK)
	1976	20	17	28	24	24	25	8	35	72	(US)
Labour force in	1960	29	46	35	48	25	21	18	48	48	(FRG)
industry, %	1977	38	49	58	51	38	31	24	48	58	(Hung.)
GDP, % in industry	1960	51	65	58	-	-	-	-	54	65	(CSSR)
	1978	52	60	47	62	55	58	-	42	62	(GDR)
GDP, % in agricult.	1960	23	13	20	-	-	-	-	6	n/m	
	1978	16	9	15	10	18	15	-	3	18	(Bulg.)
Literacy, %	1960	98	99	98	99	85	99	-	99	100	
	1970	98	n/a	99	99	91 [1]	98	-	99	100	
Telephones	1966	41	105	56	75	-	-	-	108	481	(US)
per 1000 pop.	1975	76	177	100	150	88	56	-	318	697	(US)
Newspaper circ.	1960	145	236	143	456 [1]	182	147	47 [1]	307	477	(Swe.)
per 1000 pop.	1975	248	300	233	463	232	129 [1]	46	312	572	(Swe.)
TV receivers	1965	66	149	81	188	23	26	1	193	362	(US)
per 1000 pop.	1975	180	249	223	302	173	121	2	307	571	(US)

[1] Dates may be approximate. The most recent Romanian data on urbanization were gathered in 1971 and *not* in 1976 and the East German data on newspaper circulation were collected in 1965 rather than 1960. The Bulgarian data on literacy were gathered in 1965 rather than 1960 and the Romanian and Albanian data on newspaper circulation are from 1974 and 1965 respectively.

Source: Taylor and Hudson (1972); Taylor and Jodice (1983a, 1983b).

According to a recent study (Welzel 1994, 56), dictatorships are not only less developed than democracies; they also tend to be less stable. Central and Eastern Europe may not be the best testing ground for such hypotheses, but – if taken at face value – our indicators of socioeconomic development lend support to the notion that a high level of economic development is conducive to rejection of totalitarianism and acceptance of democratization (see table 4.1).

*

Several inferences may be drawn on the basis of the socioeconomic indicators above. It is readily apparent that communist East Europe trails behind the industrial countries of the West. It is rare for the East European countries to come out at the very top of the list of socioeconomic indicators or to outdo West Germany, which entered the post-war era in a state of devastation and destruction much like that of Central and Eastern Europe; and when the East European countries actually rank at the top of the list, it is not necessarily an indicator that they are ahead of Western Europe, the United States and the British Commonwealth. The large share of industrial workers in the Hungarian labour force in 1978 (58 per cent) and the huge industrial output in the GDR, Bulgaria and Romania as of 1978 (62 per cent, 55 per cent and 58 per cent of the GDP respectively) testify to rapid social transformation and economic development, particularly compared to pre-war data (Hellén 1996) and also compared to the first decades of the post-war era (see table 4.1). The data also serve as a reminder that Eastern Europe did not provide fertile ground for what is sometimes referred to as the post-industrial society with its emphasis on service production and small-scale enterprises.[29]

It was the Soviet model of modernization of the late 1920s and 1930s, with its emphasis on industrialization, urbanization, collectivization and secularization that provided the initial impetus for the social transformation of Eastern Europe. This model lost part of its attraction, even on the local communists who had promoted it, when – after Stalin's death – the Soviet leaders openly admitted that there might be more roads than one leading to socialism, but it was never entirely abandoned. Industry in general, and huge industrial conglomerates in particular, were promoted at the expense of the agricultural sector; collective farming was at the very least preferred to private farming and religion was at best tolerated. The net result was an unprecedented social transformation of Eastern Europe with the exception of Albania which rejected one socialist partnership after the other – first with Yugoslavia (1948), then with the Soviet Union (1961) and subsequently with China (1977–78) – only in order to withdraw into splendid and self-imposed isolation as the only 'true exponent of socialism'.[30]

The East European countries lag considerably behind West Germany with respect to key developmental indicators such as the urban–rural dimension. But the differences between the 'accident–prone' Central European countries and Moscow's loyal allies on the Balkan are *not* entirely straightforward. As of the early 1960s, Bulgaria and Romania were less urban and more rural than Poland, Hungary and the GDR and basically on a par with Czechoslovakia with its pre-war record as a leading industrial nation. By 1976 Moscow's Balkan allies had caught up with Hungary and the GDR and surpassed Poland and Czecho-slovakia with respect to urbanization.

The impact of the pre-war industrial heritage is brought out by statistics on the labour force in industry, where Czechoslovakia consistently ranks at the very top along with East Germany followed by (1960), and subsequently surpassed by Hungary, (1977). Poland has a higher percentage of industrial employment than either of the two Balkan countries, but it is worth noting that the distances between Poland on the one hand and Bulgaria and Romania on the other are considerably smaller than the distances between Poland and its Central European neighbours.

The remaining indicators of economic development are of little use in helping us identify a clear-cut North–South divide.[31] Bulgaria appears to have a problem with illiteracy not shared by any of the other countries except Yugoslavia (Hellén 1996) and, in an East European context, Poland seems to have little cause for celebration when it comes to telephones, newspaper circulation and television sets per capita. Poland improves its standing over time by impressive margins, but it nevertheless finds itself either on a par with or outdone by Bulgaria and at quite a distance from the other countries of Central Europe.

*

At this stage of the enquiry, we would seem to have at least three options. We could reject our findings as based on gross, crude and unreliable indicators. We could reconsider our definition of Central Europe – East Germany, Poland, Hungary and Czechoslovakia – or we could give up the notion that there is a linear relationship between economic development and political pluralism that is likely to destabilize a dictatorship, other things being equal.

The first strategy has a lot of merit to it. The *World Handbook of Political and Social Indicators* (Taylor and Hudson 1972; Taylor and Jodice 1983a; Taylor and Hudson 1983b) is no stronger than the somewhat shaky sources on which it relies,[32] including official statistics from all corners of the world, and the measures that we have selected only represent a sample of the potential indicators of socioeconomic development, but they produce a rather clear pattern that cannot be swept under the rug with impunity.

Poland *is* an outlier in the Central European camp on almost every count,[33] but the indicators we opted for are rather standard and it is indeed a moot question whether additional indicators would produce a better fit. Poland could theoretically be removed from our definition of Central Europe and for analytical purposes counted among the other East European countries, but this would be such a blatant deviation from the historically given usage of this term that it would not even be worth considering. It would seem far better to give up the notion that there is a linear relationship between economic development and political pluralism.

It is true that dictatorships tend to be poor and socioeconomic development tends to have a destabilizing impact on dictatorships. Three of the four 'accident prone' Central European countries were well off in the East European context. But the relationship is not linear. If it had been linear, Poland would not have remained a constant problem for the Kremlin from 1956 onwards. Nor would Poland have developed into the leading champion of political pluralism in Eastern Europe that it did in the latter part of the 1980s. This is a role that the theory would have assigned to the more advanced Central European countries such as Czechoslovakia.

A comparison between the Polish and the Czechoslovak cases is in fact particularly instructive. It deals a blow, not only to the socioeconomic theory of political development, but to yet another of the many current theories about democratization in Eastern Europe — the notion that the current steps towards democracy are a function of previous exposure to democracy between the two world wars and then again in the aftermath of the Second World War (Berglund and Dellenbrant 1994c). While Poland succumbed to authoritarian strongman rule in 1926, Czechoslovakia had come out of the inter-war period as the sole Central and East European democratic survivor. While communism was literally imposed on Poland by high-handed Soviet tactics in 1947, Czechoslovakia's transition to popular democracy in 1948–49 had at least had an element of free choice and constitutionality attached to it. While Poland was treated as no more and no less than a Russian fiefdom until 1956, Czechoslovakia was held on a much longer leash, at least until Alexander Dubček's experiment in 'socialism with a human face' in the spring and summer of 1968. And yet it was Poland, and not Czechoslovakia, that set the avalanche rolling in the summer of 1989. It may be that politics matters after all.

Politics Did Matter, Even There and Then

Even dictators are not free to do as they please. They operate under a variety of domestic and external constraints. In the early history of the so-called popular democracies, the external constraints assumed particular importance. The ruling elites of Central and Eastern Europe felt compelled to embark on a programme of rapid social transformation, featuring all the components familiar from the Soviet experiment in modernization of the late 1920s and early 1930s in order to lay the foundations for a modern society. The implementation of this programme had been preceded by a high-handed approach towards the political opposition which left the communist parties firmly in command.

These measures were received with varying degrees of enthusiasm – or rather lack thereof – by the peoples of Eastern Europe who once again gained some political relevance with the transition from Stalinism to neo-Stalinism in the Soviet Union. The indicators at hand are admittedly gross and beset with even more severe reliability problems than the socioeconomic data in table 4.1, but nevertheless produce a surprisingly clear picture of Central and Eastern Europe during three decades of communist rule.

In Hungary, which had a particularly intransigent communist regime, discontent built up to the point of producing the first large-scale, nationwide uprising in the history of the Soviet bloc. The uprising or counter-revolution of November 1956 was put down by the Soviet Union, which installed a communist government that pledged allegiance to the Soviet brand of Marxism–Leninism. The loss of human lives was staggering (table 4.2) and the clocks were turned backwards. Janos Kádár, Moscow's choice for prime minister after the invasion, eventually managed to wash off the stigma of treason associated with his name and ended up as a somewhat benign father figure in Hungarian politics. The strategy he opted for was one of gradual reform. The emphasis was on economic rather than political reform. In the mid-1970s, a decade of economic reforms had produced an extremely stable political system with few, if any, outward signs of underlying political unrest (table 4.2). By the mid 1980s, the political reform process was gaining momentum but in an orderly fashion, very much marked by the trauma of 1956 (Hellén 1996).

Table 4.2 Indicators of political stability for Central and Eastern Europe

		Pol.	CSSR	Hung.	GDR	Bulg.	Rom.	Alb.	Port.	FRG
Protest	1948-77	97	282	28	58	8	26	1	246	300
demonstr.	1970-77	22	20	1	6	0	5	0	215	57
Pol. strikes	1948-77	19	39	24	47	1	2	-	35	22
	1970-77	9	1	0	0	0	1	-	23	1
Riots	1948-77	82	68	32	70	10	26	1	187	143
	1970-77	6	3	1	0	0	0	0	146	16
Deaths from	1948-77	575	101	40010	140	-	-	782	66	61
pol. violence	1970-77	22	2	0	0	-	-	0	40	43
Regime supp.	1948-77	65	54	29	60	22	12	5	43	84
demonstr.	1970-77	9	21	12	13	13	5	0	22	6
Political	1948-77	31131	57	2943	6252	41	40	5345	0	-
executions	1970-77	0	0	0	0	0	0	1	0	-

Source: Taylor and Jodice (1983a, 1983b).

In Poland, the widespread dissatisfaction with the communist regime and its Soviet allies resulted in a number of strikes, demonstrations and riots staged by the very working class, whose interests the regime was supposed to protect; and the regime was gradually forced to renege on some of its pet projects, including the collectivization of agricultural land and the aggressive campaign against religion. The latter is hardly surprising. An anti-religious appeal is not a vote or sympathy winning proposal in a deeply Catholic country such as Poland. The former is understandable in the light of the widespread opposition against collectivization throughout Poland. But the fact that Poland was the only East European country to come out of communism with well over 80 per cent of its agricultural sector in private hands nevertheless testifies to the resilience of the political opposition in Poland (Grzybowski 1994a). Table 4.2 does not cover the political turmoil that was to accompany the encounter between the communist regime and Solidarity from 1979 until the breakdown of communism in 1989–90, but it does supply plenty of evidence of turmoil in Poland from 1948 and onwards. Poland actually stands out as the East European champion of protest demonstrations, political strikes and riots all the way through the 1970s. In this respect, Poland lags behind Portugal – which was in transition from authoritarianism to democracy – but there are similarities between the two countries well worth keeping in mind.

Theoretically, the leaders of Hungary and Poland could have opted for a strategy of all-out oppression and repression. This was the Stalinist strategy familiar from the late 1940s and early 1950s. But it would have been an extremely costly strategy in the sense that it was entirely contingent upon Moscow's readiness to prop up the regime by force whenever necessary. The post-Stalinist leaders of Hungary and Poland were thus well advised to try to build up a reservoir of diffuse support for the regime. To that end, they used material as well as non-material incentives. Light industry was suddenly promoted at the expense of heavy industry. Foreign capital was imported to alleviate some of the more frustrating shortages of various commodities from wheat to cars, household appliances, perfumes and *haute couture*. Nationalist and even religious sentiments were courted and in the final analysis the regime opened up a dialogue, if not with the anti-system opposition, at least with those with ties to this opposition.

Much of this applies to East Germany (GDR) and Czechoslovakia. There were efforts made to raise the standard of living. The communist regime made an attempt to appropriate the national and religious heritage, but it did not open up any kind of dialogue with the anti-system opposition until the system was on the verge of breaking down. In this sense, East Germany and Czechoslovakia remained typical neo-Stalinists dictatorships until the demise of communism.

The data at hand suggest that the communist regimes of East Germany and Czechoslovakia also had their fair share of protest demonstrations, political strikes and riots to cope with. But in the 1970s – after the Prague Spring – things seem to have settled down just as they did in Hungary. But unlike Hungary, East Germany and Czechoslovakia had a firm commitment to the political and economic status quo; and unlike the Hungarians, the East Germans, the Czechs and the Slovaks resigned themselves to their fate.

Though a showcase socialist economy, East Germany never lived up to the standards set by its affluent West German neighbour (table 4.1). The existence of an alternative, economically successful German state – which laid claim to the entire German national heritage – put the GDR in a rather precarious position. The construction of the Berlin wall and the fortification of the border between East and West Germany were designed to stop the exodus out of East Germany, but it did not enhance the prestige of the GDR. In the 1970s and 1980s a great deal of time and energy was devoted to promoting a separate East German kind of national consciousness, but these efforts met with limited success (Berglund 1994). The number of applications for one-way exit visas to the Federal Republic kept mounting; the number of dissidents shipped to West Germany in exchange for hard currency or other shortage commodities increased from one year to the other and the police and the courts kept clamping down on any sign of political unrest (Eisenfeld 1995, 202–3).

Czechoslovakia's dissidents were in an even less enviable position in the sense that they did not have anyone to bail them out, nor anywhere to go in the unlikely event that they were to be granted exit visas. When faced with the uncomfortable choice between compliance and all the sanctions that a totalitarian regime can bring to bear on disloyal citizens, many of them opted for what became known as internal exile, i. e. formal compliance but internal rejection of everything the regime stood for. This reduced the number of outspoken dissidents to a trickle, but it did not do much for the legitimacy of the regime. The relative affluence (table 4.1) probably helped preserve social and political stability, but communism was generally perceived as an impediment to economic growth rather than as a prerequisite for economic development (Berglund and Aarebrot 1996); the system came tumbling down within little more than a week, as soon as it had been made abundantly clear that the Soviet Union was not going to stage a rerun of the dramatic events of 1968.

With few recorded protest demonstrations, strikes or riots before 1970, and hardly any thereafter, Bulgaria, Romania and, for that matter, Albania – the *enfant terrible* of Eastern Europe – stand out as extremely stable Stalinist or neo-Stalinist dictatorships (cf. figure 4.1). But what this is attributable to is a moot question: a climate of unprecedented repression, a feudal or semi-feudal heritage, poverty or – perhaps most likely – a combination of these three factors.

*

The bottomline, however, is that the history of communist Central and Eastern Europe is that of the ruling Marxist–Leninist parties. Theirs was the choice between Soviet-style Marxism–Leninism or careful reform; and in the event that they opted for reform, it was up to them to make the reforms palatable or at least acceptable to their Soviet mentors. Even though a constant hotbed for political dissent, Poland would not have become a champion for pluralism in the mid 1980s if the ruling Marxist–Leninist party had not been susceptible to dialogue and bent on compromise. And even though Hungary had become an emerging market economy by the mid-1980s, the ruling Hungarian communist party did not have to give up its self-assumed power monopoly. In theory, there was always yet another option – what became known as the Chinese solution after the dramatic events on Beijing's Tien an Minh Square, when the Chinese political establishment clamped down on the democratic movement in the night of 4–5 June 1989.

Moscow had been known to encourage such drastic methods against political oppositions within the socialist bloc and the principle of socialist solidarity gave Moscow *carte blanche* to initiate punitive expeditions against allies who failed to supress the anti-system opposition on their own, like Hungary in 1956 and Czechoslovakia in 1968. But, until the introduction of *glasnost* and *perestroika* by Gorbachev, the Soviet Union had had little cause to interfere in the internal affairs of the diehard neo-Stalinist regimes of Central and Eastern Europe. It was the cautious, gradual, but nevertheless conspicuous withdrawal of Soviet support from faithful allies like East Germany, Czechoslovakia, Bulgaria and Romania as part-and-parcel of a piecemeal re-evaluation of Russia's foreign policy objectives rather than the Polish and Hungarian examples that undermined the position of Erich Honecker, Miloš Jakeš, Todor Zhivkov and Nicolae Ceauşescu (see figure 4.2).

East Germany, Czechoslovakia and Bulgaria were at the very front line of the Warsaw Pact. From the Soviet point of view, it was imperative that these countries could be counted upon to fulfil their military obligations within the Warsaw Pact to the letter in the event of an escalation of the cold war into open confrontation between the two opposing military alliances. The emphasis was on conformity with the Soviet model of totalitarianism, which carried over well into the Gorbachev era of *glasnost* and *perestroika*. Poland, Hungary and, for that matter, Romania were further removed from the front line and could thus be given more latitude for deviations from the Soviet model. In Romania, this resulted in an extremely harsh totalitarian communist regime of an almost sultanistic flavour (Eisenstadt 1963) pursuing a maverick foreign policy. In Poland and Hungary, the long Soviet leash eventually resulted in authoritarian communist regimes bent on compromise and dialogue with the opposition.

It is questionable whether Gorbachev realized that the forces he was unleashing by lashing out publicly against the hibernating Stalinist and

Figure 4.2 Soviet security considerations and the Central and East European regimes of the late 1980s

Perceived tension - threat from NATO	Outside Soviet sphere *No control*	Front line *Tactical control important*	Logistic supply *Strategic control important*	Mobilization area *Societal control, recruitment*
Northern flank: *Weak: The Nordic balance*				Estonian SSR Latvian SSR Lithuanian SSR Perestroika *and* glasnost *with nationalist connotations*
Centre: *Strong: US troops in the Federal Republic of Germany*		GDR Czechoslovakia *Hibernating neo-Stalinist totalitarian regimes*	Poland Hungary *Authoritarian regimes bent on compromise*	Core area of the Soviet Union *Loosening of social control mechanisms through* perestroika *and* glasnost
Southern flank: *Moderate, with inter-face to Mid-Eastern conflict area*	Yugoslavia *Disintegrating totalitarian regime with elements of regional authoritarianism* Albania *Sultanistic totalitarian regime*	Bulgaria *Hibernating neo-Stalinist totalitarian regime*	Romania *Sultanistic totalitarian regime with deviant foreign policies*	

neo-Stalinist regimes of Eastern and Central Europe would reduce the ruling Marxist–Leninist parties to reformed socialist parties fighting up-hill battles against a variety of non-socialist parties, that the Warsaw Pact would be wiped out and the Soviet Union destroyed. In all likelihood, he did not; and to the extent that he did, he apparently ruled them out as unlikely options. Gorbachev was not alone. In July 1989 few, if any, Western analysts had gone on record predicting the demise of communism in Soviet-dominated Central and Eastern Europe within less than six months; and even in retrospect it is somehow mind-boggling that it did not take more time to undo what had been built over almost half a century. The implication is, of course, that the communist regimes of Central and Eastern Europe had much less diffuse support and much less legitimacy and relied on repression to a much larger extent than had been generally assumed in the West.[34]

Notes

1. The Molotov–Ribbentrop Pact between the Soviet Union and Nazi Germany of 1939 had put the Baltic states – Estonia, Latvia and Lithuania – squarely within the Soviet sphere of

influence, and they were formally integrated into the Soviet Union after a series of referenda in the winter and spring of 1940 under close supervision by the Red Army and the Soviet security forces. The ties between the Soviet Union and its three new republics were temporarily severed by the unilateral German declaration of war against the Soviet Union in June 1940, and the Red Army did not regain control of the Baltic area until late 1944 and early 1945.

2. The last constitution of the now defunct German Democratic Republic thus referred to the 'eternal friendship and alliance' with the people of the now equally defunct Soviet Union.

3. This somewhat awkward concept was coined in order to emphasize that these countries were neither 'bourgeois' democracies of the liberal capitalist variety nor advanced 'socialist' democracies of the Soviet variety. But the Soviet and East European approach to the concept was not entirely without ambiguities. There were those like Varga (1947) and Trainin (1947) who used the term to denote the transitional period between bourgeois and socialist forms of government in Eastern Europe in the late 1940s and early 1950s. There were those like Farbierov (1949) and Mankovsky (1951) who perceived popular democracy as just another form of the dictatorship of the proletariat, though originally less advanced than the Soviet model. And there were finally the adherents of the two-stage revolutionary theory who joined Sobolew (1951) in questioning the socialist nature of the popular-democratic revolutions of the mid-1940s.

4. In the Soviet Union, there was traditionally a front of communists and non-communists, but only prior to the elections. The national front of the communist Central and East European countries was a forum not only for political parties, but also for officially recognized mass organizations like trade unions, youth organizations and women's movements, all of which had parliamentary representation in their own right (Berglund and Dellenbrant 1994b).

5. Many of the representatives of the other social movements, say the trade union movement, were also card-carrying communist party members; and the ruling Marxist-Leninist party could, therefore, rest assured that its leading role would not be questioned by the patriotic or national front (Berglund and Dellenbrant 1994b).

6. The Council of State – a miniature parliament of sorts – assumed responsibility for the legislative work when the parliament was not in session (Berglund 1994).

7. There are numerous indications of the high-handed approach of the Red Army and Soviet security forces in Central and Eastern Europe of the late 1940s and early 1950s, paricularly in Poland which was basically treated as a Russian fiefdom (Brzezinski 1965, 1989; Hellén 1996).

8. It was in fact a joint Warsaw Pact intervention, including military units from all Warsaw Pact countries with the exception of Romania.

9. The Romanian party leader Nicolae Ceauşescu embarked on a course that emphasized Romania's independence from Moscow in foreign affairs. The Romanian decision *not* to participate in the Warsaw Pact intervention in Czechoslovakia in August 1968 contributed towards enhancing the prestige of the Ceauşescu regime in the West. But, with the Stalinist policies he pursued at home, Ceauşescu could hardly be accused of deviating from the orthodox party line.

10. This is certainly more than Zbigniew K. Brzezinski had when writing his book, *The Grand Failure: The Birth and Death of Communism in the Twentieth Century*, New York, Macmillan, which was published in 1989, but had clearly been written well before it became apparent that Central and Eastern Europe was about to break out of the Soviet fold.

11. There are deviations from this rule, but they are all associated with atypical communist leaders such as Imre Nagy of Hungary (1956) and Alexander Dubček of Czechoslovakia (1968).

12. This is one leg of the so-called convergence theory, where the two super powers of the 1960s are cast as drifting towards one another with the USSR adopting at least some of the

pluralistic features of the US and with the US espousing at least parts of the Soviet philosophy of social planning (cf Huntington and Brzezinski 1965).

13. The transition from Stalinism to neo-Stalinism reduced the penalties attached to opposition but the state nevertheless had an array of awesome sanctions at its disposal.

14. Linz's full definition of authoritarianism is cast in terms that would seem to rule out the Soviet Union and its East European allies. He describes authoritarian regimes as 'political systems with limited, not responsible, political pluralism; without elaborate and guiding ideology (but with distinctive mentalities); without intensive nor extensive political mobilization (except some points in their development); and in which a leader (or occasionally a small group) exercises power within formally ill-defined limits but actually quite predictable ones' (Linz 1964, 297).

15. Gomułka and his associates had been expelled from the ruling United Workers and Peasant Party in 1949 on charges of nationalistic leanings. Initially though Gomułka was not even arrested (he was taken into custody in 1951) and never tried. There were no show trials in Poland (Brzezinski 1965, 96).

16. The membership dues constituted 1 per cent of the monthly wages or salaries.

17. Solidarity chose to interpret the referendum as a vote of confidence in the Jaruzelski government and called on its followers to abstain from voting. With an abstention rate of one third, the turnout did not meet the minimum percentage of eligible voters.

18. Solidarity gained all the contested seats with the exception of one seat which went to an independent candidate (Grzybowski 1994a).

19. Kádár, who was a minister in Nagy's government and apparently had advance knowledge of the Soviet decision to intervene, dropped out of sight for several days prior to the intervention, only to reappear as Moscow's choice for prime minister when the fighting had subsided.

20. The dialogue did not open up, nor did the negotiations get under way, until August 1989, when Károly Grósz had been replaced at the bargaining table by a reformer (Jenkins 1992, 126).

21. In his article, 'East Germany: Dissenting Views during the Last Decade' in Tökés, ed., *Oppositions in Eastern Europe* (1979), Werner Volkmer makes a survey of the anti-system opposition in the GDR, which basically remained valid throughout the 1980s.

22. Letting the East Germans out was a breach of the 'socialist solidarity' that had been confirmed in formal treaties, still in effect in the summer of 1989, between East Germany on the one hand and Poland and Hungary on the other.

23. According to Dawisha (1984), the evidence would seem to suggest that the Soviet leaders were convinced that Czechoslovakia would remain within the Warsaw Pact even under Dubček, but used the fear of a Czechoslovak alliance with West Germany and the US as a pretext for the decision to invade.

24. Though a member of the Warsaw Pact, Romania did not take part in the military campaign against Czechoslovakia, nor in verbal campaign preceding the military operation (Bankowicz 1994a; see also footnote 9).

25. The open competition in the Romanian Communist Party in 1979, when Konstantin Privulescu, ran against Nicolae Ceauşescu, is one of the most conspicuous cases (East 1992, 138).

26. The Bulgarian Zhivkov regime relied on concentration camps as a final recourse in its attempts to curb potential opposition (East 1992, 23) and *Securitate* – Ceauşescu's paramilitary security forces – had a well deserved reputation for brutality (Berglund and Dellenbrant 1994c).

27. Once a devout Stalinist ally of the Soviet Union, Albania had broken out of the Soviet camp in the wake of the twentieth party congress of the CPSU, which had initiated a cautious policy of de-Stalinization. Albania subsequently gravitated towards the Chinese position in the Sino–Soviet conflict, only to be rejected by its Chinese allies in the late 1980s. This marked the beginning of an almost total isolation from the world communist

movement in the late 1980s which put Albania in the rather uncomfortable position of being the only spokesman of 'true communism' in an antagonistic world.

28. We are basically referring to the transition from *Gestaltung* to *Verwaltung*.

29. The emerging private service sectors in Poland and Hungary were admittedly less likely to get integrated into the official statistics than officially approved lines of work, but it is also worth remembering that the private sector only provided an additional source of income for many of those thus employed (see above).

30. Though also outside the Soviet bloc, Yugoslavia adopted a policy of industrialization which put it on a par with Russia's two Balkán allies (Hellén 1996).

31. The time series on industrial versus agricultural GDP are unfortunately incomplete and thus cannot be taken into account here.

32. The slight – but nevertheless significant – discrepancies between the data on the 1960s as reported in the 1972 and 1983 versions of the *World Handbook of Political and Social Indicators* do have something to say about the quality of the data.

33. The low degree of urbanization in Czechoslovakia – presumably an artefact of the unequal level of development in Czechia (Bohemia and Moravia) and Slovakia – constitutes the only exception from this rule.

34. There are many kinds of repression that do not lend themselves to quantification in the same straightforward way as the number of political executions or number of political prisoners over time such as thwarted career ambitions, forced adoptions and character assassination.

References

Aarebrot, Frank and Sten Berglund (1995), 'Statehood, Secularization, Cooptation: Explaining Democratic Survival in Inter-War Europe – Stein Rokkan's Conceptual Map Revisited', in Stefan Immerfall and Peter Steinbach, eds, *Historisch-vergleichende Makrosoziologie: Stein Rokkan – der Beitrag eines Kosmopoliten aus der Peripherie*, Published as Special Issue No. 2, Vol. 20, of *Historical Social Research*.

Almond, Gabriel A. and G. Bingham Powell Jr (1978), *Comparative Politics: A Developmental Approach*, 2nd edition, Boston, Little, Brown.

Bankowicz, Marek (1994a), 'Czechoslovakia: From Masaryk to Havel', in Sten Berglund and Jan Åke Dellenbrant, eds, *The New Democracies in Eastern Europe: Party Systems and Political Cleavages*, 2nd edition, Aldershot, Edward Elgar.

— (1994b), 'Bulgaria: The Continuing Revolution, in Sten Berglund and Jan Åke Dellenbrant, eds, *opus cited*.

Berglund, Sten (1994), 'The Breakdown of the German Democratic Republic', in Sten Berglund and Jan Åke Dellenbrant, eds, *opus cited*.

Berglund, Sten and Frank Aarebrot (1996), 'The View fron Central and Eastern Europe', in Oscar Niedermayer and Richard Sinnott, eds, *Public Opinion and Internationalized Governance*, Volume 2 of the Beliefs in Government Project, Oxford, Oxford University Press.

Berglund, Sten and Jan Åke Dellenbrant (1994a), 'The Breakdown of Communism in Eastern Europe', in Sten Berglund and Jan Åke Dellenbrant, eds, *opus cited*.

— (1994b), 'The Failure of Popular Democracy', in Sten Berglund and Jan Åke Dellenbrant, eds, *opus cited*.

— (1994c), 'Prospects for Democracy in Eastern Europe', in Sten Berglund and Jan Åke Dellenbrant, eds, *opus cited*.

Brzezinski, Zbigniev K. (1965), *The Soviet Bloc: Unity and Conflict*, New York, Frederick A. Praeger.

— (1989), *The Grand Failure: The Birth of Communism in the Twentieth Century*, New York, Praeger.

Dawisha, Karen (1984), *The Kremlin and the Prague Spring*, Berkeley and Los Angeles, University of California Press.

Dellenbrant, Jan Åke (1994a), 'The Re-Emergence of Multi-Partyism in the Baltic States, in Sten Berglund and Jan Åke Dellenbrant, eds, *opus cited*.

— (1994b), 'Romania: The Slow Revolution', in Sten Berglund and Jan Åke Dellenbrant, eds, *opus cited*.

Deppe, R. and D. Hoss (1989), *Arbeitspolitik im Staatssozialismus: Zwei Varianten – DDR und Ungarn*, Frankfurt am Main, Campus.

East, Roger (1992), *Revolutions in Eastern Europe*, London and New York, Pinter Publishers.

Eisenfeld, Bernd (1995), 'Die Ausreisebewegung – eine Erscheinungsform wider-ständigen Verhaltens', in Ulrike Poppe, Rainer Eckert and Ilko-Sascha Kowalczuk, eds, *Zwischen Selbstbehauptung und Anpassung: Formen des Wider-standes und Opposition in der DDR*, Berlin, Ch. Links Verlag.

Eisenstadt, Schmul (1963), *The Political Systems of Empires*, London, Macmillan.

Farbierov, N. (1949), *Gosudarstvennoe pravo stran narodnoi demokratii* (The State Law of the Popular Democracies), Moscow, Politizdat.

Friedrich, Carl and Zbigniev K. Brzezinski (1965), *Totalitarian Dictatorship and Autocracy*, Boston, Harvard University Press.

Gati, Charles (1986), *Hungary and the Soviet Bloc*, Durham, NC, Duke University Press.

Gilberg, Trond (1992), 'The Multiple Legacies of History: Romania in the Year 1990', in Joseph Held, ed., *The Columbia History of Eastern Europe in the Twentieth Century*, New York, Columbia University Press.

Grzybowski, Marian (1994a), 'Poland: Towards Overdeveloped Pluralism', in Sten Berglund and Jan Åke Dellenbrant, eds, *opus cited*.

— (1994b), The Transition to Competitive Pluralism in Hungary, in Sten Berlund and Jan Åke Dellenbrant, eds, *opus cited*.

Hellén, Tomas (1996), *Shaking Hands with the Past: Origins of the Political Right in Central Europe*, Helsinki, The Finnish Society of Sciences and Letters and the Finnish Academy of Science and Letters.

Huntington, Samuel P. and Zbigniev K. Brzezinski (1965), *Political Power: USA USSR*, New York, Praeger.

— (1968), *Political Order in Changing Societies*, New Haven, Yale University Press.

Jenkins, Robert M. (1992), 'Society and Regime Transition in East–Central Europe', in György Szoboszlai, ed., *Flying Blind*, Budapest, Hungarian Political Science Association.

Kuusinen, Otto Ville (1959), *Osnovy Marksizma–Leninizma* (The Foundations of Marxism–Leninism), Moscow, Politizdat. Produced by a collective of authors under the guidance of Kuusinen.

Linz, Juan (1964), 'An Authoritarian Regime: Spain', in Erik Allardt and Yrjö Littunen, eds, *Cleavages, Ideologies and Party Systems: Contributions to Comparative Political Sociology*, Helsinki, Transactions of the Westermarck Society, Vol. X.

– (1974), 'Totalitarian and Authoritarian Regimes', in Fred I. Greenstein and Nelson W. Polsby, eds, *Handbook of Political Science*, Vol. III.

Mankovsky, B. S. (1951), 'Sushchnost yevropeiskikh narodno-demokraticheskikh gosudarstv', (The Essence of European Popular Democracies) in *Nektorye voprosy gosudarstva i prava stran demokratii* (Selected Questions of State and Law in Popular Democracy), Moscow, Nauka.

Nowak, Jerzy Robert (1984), *Węgry wychodzenie z kryzysu* (Hungary Coming out of Crisis), Warszawa, Książka i Wiedza.

Parland, Thomas (1993), *The Rejection in Russia of Totalitarian Socialism and Liberal Democracy: A Study of the Russian New Right*, Helsinki, The Finnish Society of Sciences and Letters.

Sartori, Giovanni (1965), *Democratic Theory*, New York, Frederick A. Praeger.

— (1987), *The Theory of Democracy Revisited*, Chatham, NJ, Chatham House Publishers.

Sobolew, A. (1951), 'Demokracja ludowa jako forma politycznej organizacji spoleczenstwa (Popular Democracy as a Form of Political Organization of Society)', *Nowe Drogi*, no. 5.

Taylor, Charles Lewis and Michael C. Hudson, eds, (1972), *World Handbook of Political and Social Indicators*, 2nd edition, New Haven, Yale University Press.

— and David A. Jodice, eds, (1983a), *World Handbook of Political and Social Indicators: Cross-National Attributes and Rates of Change*, Vol. 1, 3rd edition, New Haven, Yale University Press.

— , eds, (1983b), *World Handbook of Political and Social Indicators: Political Protest and Government Change*, Vol. 2, 3rd edition, New Haven, Yale University Press.

Tökes, R., ed, (1979), *Oppositions in Eastern Europe*, London and New York, Macmillan.

Trainin, I. P. (1947), 'Demokratiya osobogo tipa´, (Democracy of a Special Type) *Sovetskoe gosudarstvo i pravo* (Soviet State and Law).

Varga, E. (1947), 'Demokratiya novogo tipa (Democracy of a New type)', Mirovoe *khoziaistvo i mirovaya politika* (World Economy and World Politics), no. 3.

Volkmer, W. (1979), 'East Germany: Dissenting Views during the Last Decade', in R. Tökés, ed, *Oppositions in Eastern Europe*, London and New York, Macmillan.

Welzel, Christian (1994), 'Systemwechsel in der globalen Systemkonkurrenz: Ein evolutionsteoretischer Erklärungsversuch, in Wolfgang Merkel, ed, *Systemwechsel 1: Theorien Ansätze und Konzeptionen*, Opladen, Leske & Budrich.

5. Democracy: The Second Coming

The Return of Pluralism

The first free or almost free elections in Poland in well over 40 years were held on 4 June 1989. By the beginning of 1990, Moscow's allies in Central and Eastern Europe had all pledged themselves to parliamentary democracy and a market economy. The transition was not only very quick. It was basically orderly and peaceful. When challenged by widespread popular unrest, Ceauşescu was the only East European communist leader to make a serious attempt to hold on to power by force. The net result was a bloody civil war between Ceauşescu loyalist forces and the bulk of the army – which sided with the rebels – between Christmas and the New Year of 1989–90.

The movement towards political and economic reform in the Baltic states was parallel to that of Central and Eastern Europe. Reform communists played an important role, particularly at the outset of the process of democratization, but the problems were of a different magnitude from those confronting the political leaders of the Warsaw Pact countries. If the Baltic republics were allowed to break out of the Soviet Union, it might jeopardize the very existence of the Union (Berglund and Dellenbrant 1994). In the final analysis, the central government in Moscow resigned itself to the fact that the Baltic republics would go their own way, but Moscow was reluctant to accept the erosion of its power base that Baltic independence would entail and the three Baltic republics did not obtain formal independence from the Soviet Union until after the abortive coup against Gorbachev by communist hard-liners in August 1991.[1]

With communism on the way out, political pluralism reasserted itself in Eastern Europe. By 1989–90, Poland and Hungary already had a long record of dialogue and negotiations between government and opposition. The communist regimes of East Germany, Czechoslovakia, Bulgaria and Romania had not cultivated such a political climate. But by the winter and spring of 1990, these countries were also heading for free and competitive elections. The situation confronting the re-enfranchised East European voters was reminiscent of that prevailing in West Germany and Italy in the immediate aftermath of the Second World War (1945–47). Totalitarianism had been defeated; proportional representation (PR) had been introduced; the threshold of represent-ation was low and the cleavage structure remained in a state of flux after almost half a decade of 'real socialism'.[2] This was a promising setting for hopeful political entrepreneurs.

The situation varied somewhat from country to country. The Hungarian parliament quickly adopted an electoral law with a number of extremely complicated provisions, including a 4 per cent threshold for parliamentary representation, designed to discourage political fragmentation (Grzybowski 1994b; Tóka 1995). Initially at least, Poland remained true to the inter-war Weimar-style concept of fairness which produced one of the most pronounced cases of extreme pluralism in the entire region. The liberal Election Law of June 1991 left the nomination of candidates in the hands of loosely organized electoral committees; and prior to the election of 27 October 1991, candidates were being run by no less than 117 such electoral committees. The vast majority of them failed to propel their respective candidates into parliament, but there were nevertheless enough winners to make for a very complicated parliamentary situation (Grzybowski 1994a). The net result was 18 different parliamentary clubs representing the three major groups of parties or political movements that have dominated Poland and most of the other East European countries ever since the breakdown of communism (see table 5.1).

In contemporary Eastern Europe there are parties with a glorious but distant past in the inter-war era and the first few years of the semi-democratic interlude in the wake of the Second World War like social democratic, Christian democratic and agrarian parties. There are parties with their ideological roots in the drawn-out communist parenthesis (1949–89) such as the reformed communist parties and their one-time partners in the building of socialism. Last but not least, there are the heirs of the socially and politically heterogeneous umbrella organizations which served as a rallying point for the anti-system opposition in the struggle against communism as of the late 1980s and early 1990s in many of the East European countries.

With a history spanning over three decades, Solidarity is the best known of these umbrella organizations (Grzybowski 1994a), but by the

Table 5.1 Parliamentary clubs in the Polish *Sejm* after the election of
27 October 1991

Party/Organization	Number of seats	Percent of seats
1. Democratic Union	62	13.5
2. Alliance of Democratic Left	59	13.0
3. Confederation for an Independent Poland	51	11.1
4. Polish Peasant Party	50	10.9
5. Christian–National Union (Catholic Electoral Action)	49	10.7
6. Alliance Centrum	42	9.1
7. Liberal–Democratic Congress	37	8.0
8. Solidarity as a Trade Union	27	5.9
9. Peasant People's Alliance	18	3.9
10. Polish Economic Programme	13	2.8
11. Polish Peasant Party Solidarity	10	2.2
12. German Minority	7	1.5
13. Christian Democratic Party	6	1.3
14. Solidarity of Labour	5	1.1
15. Christian Democracy	5	1.1
16. Polish Friends of Beer	3	0.7
17. Union for Real Politics	3	0.7
18. Party X (Tymiński)	3	0.7
19. Independents	10	2.2

Source: Gebethner and Raciborski (1992, 56); Grzybowski (1994a, 64).

late 1980s a number of East European countries had followed the
Polish example. Founded in 1979, the Hungarian Democratic Forum
(HDF) is in fact of the same vintage as Solidarity. It contributed
towards the negotiated and low-keyed demise of communism in
Hungary. In Estonia, Latvia and Lithuania so-called popular fronts
became driving forces in the struggle for national independence and
political democracy (Dellenbrant 1994a). In Czechoslovakia, Civic
Forum (Czech Republic) and Public Against Violence (Slovak
Republic) served as rallying points for the built-up discontent

Table 5.2 The results of the first and second rounds of the parliamentary elections in Hungary, March and April 1990

Party/political movement	Percentage of valid votes	
	1st round	*2nd round*
Hungarian Democratic Forum	24.7	43.0
Alliance of Free Democrats	21.4	23.8
Smallholders' Party	11.7	11.4
Hungarian Socialist Party	10.9	8.5
FIDESZ	8.9	5.4
Christian Democratic Party	6.5	5.4
HSWP	3.7	
Social Democrats	3.5	
Others	8.7	2.4

Sources: Reisch (1990); Patáki (1990); Grzybowski (1994b, 193).

unleashed by the dramatic events of November 1989. Similar comments apply to the Union of Democratic Forces (UDF) of Bulgaria (Bankowicz 1994b).

Solidarity had a field day in the partially free elections of 1989. Two and a half years later, Solidarity had split up under the impact of internal tensions and conflict, but the *Sejm* remained dominated by Solidarity splinter movements such as the Democratic Union, the Alliance Centrum and the Liberal Democratic Congress (see table 5.1).

With 168 seats out of a total of 300, Civic Forum and Public Against Violence came out as the undisputed winners of the elections to the Czechoslovak national assembly which were held in June 1990. But shortly thereafter, Civic Forum fell prey to internal conflict; and with the election of Václav Klaus, the minister of finance and the architect of Czechoslovakia's neo-liberal economic reform programme, to the position of chairman, Civic Forum developed more and more into a right-wing organization with policies rather far removed from Václav Havel's notion of 'capitalism with a human face' (*La Republica*, 21 September 1990, 20ff). In addition to political fragmentation, Czechoslovakia soon found itself under the impact of other problems: most notably the rapidly deteriorating relations between the Czech and the Slovak republics which resulted in the so-called velvet divorce of 1 January 1992.

With its distinctly patriotic and nationalistic appeal, the Hungarian Democratic Forum had always been less heterogeneous than Solidarity Civic Forum and, for that matter, the catch-all popular fronts of the Baltic countries who lost much of their importance once independence had been achieved;[3] HDF came strong and united out of the founding elections of March–April 1990 (see table 5.2).

Nevertheless, the HDF fell short of obtaining a majority in its own right. A coalition with the liberal Free Democrats would have produced a handsome parliamentary majority, but the HDF rejected this option in favour of an alliance with the Smallholders and the Christian Democrats, who were ideologically closer to the HDF than the liberal and socialist parties.[4] This conservative coalition remained in power until it lost the mandate of the voters in the May elections of 1994, which resulted in an overwhelming victory for the reform communists.

*

Strictly speaking, the new democracies in Eastern Europe are all unique. But there are, nevertheless, some differences and similarities worth mentioning. Many of the East European countries, but by no means all, had popular fronts or large-scale citizens' movements, which served as rallying points in the final struggle against communism. The struggle for democracy in Poland, Czechoslovakia and Hungary was strongly marked by Solidarity, Civic Forum, Public Against Violence and the Hungarian Democratic Forum. The popular fronts of the Baltic countries and the citizens' movements of East Germany played an equally important role in the last-ditch struggle for independence and against communism, but they all failed to defend the position of national prominence that they had at the outset (Crampton and Crampton 1996). In Bulgaria, the Union of Democratic Forces (UDF) lost the first but won the second free election in 1990 and 1991 respectively (Bankowicz 1994b).

Romania, on the other hand, did not have any such citizens' movement at all. Ion Iliescu, Ceauşescu's successor and long-time heir apparent, likes to present the National Salvation Front (NSF) as such a citizens' movement, but it is not, at least not on a par with the above popular fronts. The National Salvation Front is not a grass-roots movement. It was proclaimed by the leaders of the palace revolution against Ceauşescu, which coincided with the Bucharest uprising in December 1989; and it was successfully used in a bid to take over and appropriate the organizational infrastructure of the then ruling Communist Party (Dellenbrant 1994b).

Tables 5.1 and 5.2 make it abundantly clear that 1990 was not a good year for communists of any shade. The truth of the matter is that 1990 was a bad year for all self-confessed socialists, even for *bona fide* social democrats and not only for former communists who found the social democratic party label somehow less offensive. On the whole, the East European founding elections, i.e. the first elections under democratic rules, resulted in a gigantic swing to the right that all but wiped out the parties of the left. This was definitely the case in the Baltic republics[5] and in Central Europe with the possible exception of East Germany. But this was not the case in Bulgaria, where the reformed communist party gained a parliamentary majority in its own right; nor in Romania, where the National Salvation Front defeated the opposition by a broad margin; nor for that matter in Albania, Serbia and the former Soviet republics in the southern part of the defunct Soviet empire.

The Return to Pessimism

The East Europeans, including the Bulgarians and the Albanians, saw the demise of communism as a golden opportunity for the East European countries to take their rightful place in Europe and join West European cooperative ventures, particularly the European Community. There were frequent references on both sides of the former Iron Curtain to a new and peaceful world order with NATO providing the military deterrent needed to protect the territorial integrity of its new members. The term euro-euphoria has sometimes been used to describe the intellectual climate that prevailed in Eastern as well as Western Europe at the beginning of the 1990s; and it is not that far off the mark, even though Eastern and Western Europe both had their fair share of sceptics (Berglund and Aarebrot 1996).

Optimism, however, soon gave way to pessimism. The many similarities with the inter-war era was a source of concern to political scientists and journalists alike. We have already identified political fragmentation as a problem. In cases of extreme political pluralism such as France and Germany of the early 1930s or Poland in the early

1990s, government formation and government stability are likely to be jeopardized. In chapter 2 we made the rather obvious point that a severe economic depression – with all that this entails by way of unemployment, hardship and uncertainty – has a strongly destabilizing potential. The Great Depression of the late 1920s and early 1930s was not solely responsible for the subsequent breakdown of democracy in Weimar Germany, but it undoubtedly reduced the credibility of the democratic regime. As such, the economic crisis in post-war Eastern Europe was not enough to bring down the fledgling democracies that emerged in the wake of the war, but the crisis certainly proved to be an asset for the communists in their attempts to bring about the long sought for transformation to Soviet-style communism (see chapter 3). In a similar vein, it may be argued that the serious economic problems, which have accompanied the transition from plan to market in Eastern Europe, have an enormous destabilizing potential. Or as Stephen Fischer-Galati puts it:

> Present conditions are no better for making Eastern Europe safe for democracy than they were at the end of World War I. If economic prosperity, presumably assured by a market economy, is essential for democracy, the prospects are grim. The highly competitive capitalist economies of Western Europe, the United States, and Japan are only marginally interested in providing economic assistance or in developing markets in heavily indebted countries with worthless currencies, inefficient work forces, and obsolete industrial plants (Fischer-Galati 1992, 15).

Paradoxically enough, it may even be argued that contemporary Eastern Europe is far worse off than inter-war Eastern Europe. When measured against the standard indicators, the former stands out as much more developed than the latter. Historically speaking, Eastern Europe has never been as industrialized, as urbanized, as secularized and as well educated as it was after having emerged from almost half a century of 'real socialism'. But half a century of Soviet-style communism had also wiped out the foundations of the inter-war market economy and undermined the inter-war cleavage structure. If it is true, as Dahl (1992) and others would argue, that democracy requires a capitalist or at least a mixed economy, the new democracies of Eastern Europe are clearly in trouble. If it is also true that a country is not safe for democracy as long as its party system finds itself in a state of flux, there would seem to be even more cause for concern about Eastern

Europe. It took decades for the West European party system to settle down and freeze (Rokkan et al. 1970), and it would perhaps be unrealistic to expect this process to be more rapid in a setting with such a diffuse class structure as the former communist countries of Eastern Europe.

There are actually two stable cleavages – ethnicity and religion – in Eastern Europe, but it is a moot question whether they can provide the basis for a stable party system in a modern society and they both raise the spectre of strife and conflict. The post-war borders of Eastern Europe were redrawn by the Soviet Union to its own advantage; and there was nothing the East European countries could do about it at the time, nor, for that matter, during the cold war. There is not much they can do about the unfavourable border changes now either, short of staging a local war and risking condemnation by the international community. But there is one important difference between the new and the old set of rules in Eastern Europe. The old rules did not allow the individual East European countries to exploit ethnic tensions that risked undermining cohesion within the Warsaw Pact. The new rules do not contain any such restrictions and there have indeed been quite a few verbal skirmishes, involving individual East European countries like Romania, Hungary, Poland, Russia and Slovakia,[6] and one devastating civil war with strongly ethnic and nationalistic overtones in Bosnia, in the middle of Europe, since the breakdown of communism in 1989–90.

*

Most pieces of the obituary are already in place. But the patient – if patient it is – is still alive, perhaps even well. So far at least, there are no cases of democratic breakdown but several encouraging progress reports at hand (Wessels and Klingemann 1994). After having been criticized for mismanagement and government interference in the 1990 founding elections Romania drew favourable comments from the international election observers for smooth and fair handling of the 1992 elections (Crampton and Crampton 1996).

On a more general level, it may be noted that all the countries of Eastern Europe have had two or more parliamentary elections since the breakdown of communism in 1989–90. As a rule, these elections have been seen as fair and just. The vast majority of them have resulted in a change of guards. Of the former Warsaw Pact countries, Romania is alone *not* having experienced even a temporary shift from communism to conservatism or liberalism. The violent transition from Ceauşescu to Iliescu in 1989–90 represented a move from totalitarian to reform communism – a choice that has since been confirmed and reconfirmed by the voters. The overwhelming majority of the Warsaw Pact countries, including the Baltic states, have by now experienced at least three kinds of regimes since the late 1980s: totalitarian or authoritarian communism prior to 1989–90, a strongly non-communist right-wing government in the wake of the velvet revolution followed by the electoral victory of the reformed communists campaigning on a socialist or social democratic platform. In the light of this rather normal cyclical democratic behaviour, the unbroken success of Václav Klaus over several consecutive elections in the Czech lands stands out as quite remarkable.

This is not to say that the fears and concerns of many of our fellow political scientists are to be taken lightly. On the contrary, they stand on solid theoretical ground and must be taken quite seriously. The case for or against the new democracies in Eastern Europe is often stated in broad and sweeping terms (cf. Fischer-Galati 1992), and it would benefit from a more systematic approach to democracy at work. This is the task to which we now turn.

The Democratic Challenges Revisited

On the basis of seemingly compelling evidence, Sartori (1966, 1976) portrays political fragmentation as a bad omen for democracy. But the argument is not watertight. In a series of books and articles, Arend Lijphart (1968, 1977, 1991) identifies a number of countries (cf. chapter 2), including Belgium and the Netherlands, which stand out as stable democracies while having highly fragmented party systems. Though disintegrated all the way up to the national level, these so-called 'consociational democracies' are held together by a political culture and a set of national political elites which put a premium on elite-level cooperation across the cultural and political divides. This is in fact how we would account for the exceptional political stability in inter-war Czechoslovakia, our one and only Central and East European survivor as of 1938 (Bradley 1971, 1992; Bankowicz 1994a); and though perhaps inherently unstable, the model might still work in Central and Eastern Europe.

But political fragmentation is not a constant, given once and for all. It varies and it can be made to vary over time. It is susceptible to political manipulation and lends itself to what we would refer to as creative electoral engineering. This is exactly what happened in Poland, Bulgaria and Romania, which went into parliamentary democracy without any thresholds of representation (Crampton and Crampton 1996). The rules of the game were simply changed. In Poland, a 5 per cent threshold for individual parties and an 8 per cent threshold for electoral alliances were added to the Liberal Election Law of June 1991, which had produced one of the most highly fragmented legislatures in the entire region (cf. table 5.1), and the reform most certainly paid off. The new *Sejm* that was elected in May 1993 counted 6 as opposed to 18 political parties.[7]

Thresholds of parliamentary representation need not work as smoothly as they did in Poland; and they obviously do not constitute a guarantee against fragmentation. Political parties have been known to fall apart between elections. In this event, the threshold of representation is likely to punish some of the new parties or factions, but only at the following election, and until then the parliamentary system will have to cope with the strain that a high level of fragmentation imposes on it.

*

The breakdown of the planned economy and the transition to a market economy spelled hardship for the citizens of Eastern Europe. Prices and unemployment went up and shortages became the order of the day as all the relevant macro–economic indicators took a turn for the worse (Crampton and Crampton 1996). It is impossible to say who was most badly hurt by this economic crisis, but some general comments are in order.

Inflation, unemployment and food shortages deal a severe blow to those who are already weak and disadvantaged: people without professional training, the unemployed, the old, the young and other people on fixed incomes. The severity of the blow varies with the original resources of the individual citizens and the overall economic standing of their respective countries. The transition to capitalism was particularly smooth in East Germany which was bailed out by West Germany and particularly rough in Albania and Romania which came out of communism in profound economic crisis (Gilberg 1992). The mass exodus of Albanians into neighbouring Italy, when the borders opened up in the summer of 1990, testifies to the severity of the crisis in this underdeveloped country in the European periphery. The Romanians had been subjected to a harsh austerity programme, imposed by the Ceauşescu government in a prestige-related effort to pay off foreign debt at a more rapid pace than required by the creditors which had literally pushed them to the brink of starvation (Gilberg 1992; Dellenbrant 1994b).

The situation was much better in the other East European countries, particularly in Poland and Hungary which had embarked on the road of economic reform well before the breakdown of the communist regimes. But that was not enough to protect them from the classical East European syndrome, including drastically falling gross domestic products (GDP) and skyrocketing inflation, during the first few years after the transition to a market economy.

Things have improved dramatically since 1990–91, but not to the point of reducing the importance of redistributive issues on the political agenda. The breakdown of the communist-style welfare state and the gradual emergence of a new and conspicuously wealthy entrepreneurial class, often with ties to the old communist *nomenklatura*, have paved the way for a new kind of left/right cleavage revolving around attitudes towards capitalism and economic reform. To the extent that the appearance of this left/right cleavage spells polarization, it may very well be detrimental to the stability of the democratic regime. But it may also be interpreted as a natural expansion of the left/right spectrum and thus as a return to pre-war normalcy.

It may in fact be argued that the party systems that emerged in Eastern Europe in the immediate aftermath of communism had something truly provisional about them. There were parties of the right and parties of the extreme right; there were conservative parties and some liberal parties. But there were virtually no parties of the left, nor any parties of the extreme left. This was, of course, a byproduct of the anti-communist backlash that swept over most of Eastern Europe in 1989–90, but it was not likely to last under conditions of competitive pluralism. In such a setting, the governing right-wing coalitions, most of which embarked on a programme of rapid economic reform, were bound to be challenged from the left sooner or later.

The East European parties of the left and the extreme left have their ideological roots within the defunct or reformed Marxist–Leninist parties and are no strangers to appealing to nationalistic sentiments, but the recent revival of the left/right cleavage would seem to imply that the ethnic and nationalistic cleavages no longer dominate to the extent that they did in the immediate aftermath of the recent East European revolution, when even a faint smell of socialism was enough to scare the voters off.

The Transition as Perceived by East European Polls

To the extent that modern political survey research had been carried out in Eastern Europe before the revolution of 1989–90, it had been an instrument of the ruling Marxist–Leninist parties, who disposed of the findings as they saw fit.[8] The transition from communism to parliamentary democracy and a market economy spelled fundamental change and opened up the entire region for mass surveys of the kind familiar from the Western hemisphere. There is now an array of surveys available for secondary analyses, ranging from country-specific surveys commissioned by parties and/or newspapers relying on the many polling institutes that have been founded in Eastern Europe during the last few years to cross-country studies covering the entire region or several of the so-called post-communist countries.

The latter are of particular relevance to students of comparative politics. We will mainly rely on the data compiled by the European Commission within the framework of the European Integration Studies and the Eurobarometers East, but the first indicator to be displayed is in fact derived from another comparative data set: the Times–Mirror survey of 1990 which included an item on the crucial question of how to deal with the instruments of the old regime.

The outcome is surprisingly moderate (see figure 5.1). Eighty per cent or more of Poles and Hungarians say they are willing to keep people of the old regime if they are any good. The Bulgarians, the Czechs and the Slovaks are significantly less inclined to let bygones be bygones. But with some 57–62 per cent of the respondents in Bulgaria and Czechoslovakia coming out in favour of the pragmatic solution to this rather crucial problem facing the new democracies in Eastern Europe, the overall impression is indeed one of moderation.

Generally speaking, the new democracies of Eastern Europe adopted a lenient policy towards former top-level communist fellow travellers, but East Germany and Czechoslovakia did not. East Germany was not covered by the Times–Mirror survey, so we do not know for sure how

Figure 5.1 Percentage of respondents who would keep top people of the old regime if they were any good

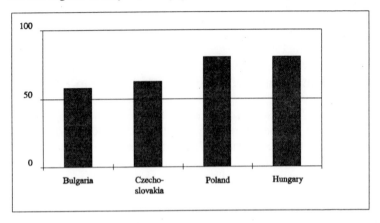

the East German voters felt about their former rulers back in 1989–90. We do know that the first and last freely elected *Volkskammer* introduced legislation designed to punish the former members and collaborators of *Stasi*, the once-omnipotent East German security police, a policy which carried over into the enlarged *Bundesrepublik* (Croan 1992; East 1992). We know that the Czech National Assembly enacted an even more arbitrary set of rules designed to combat the old ideological foe (East 1992; Wolchik 1992); and, considering the outcome of the Times–Mirror survey, we would be inclined to interpret this as an elite rather than a grass-roots reaction. This was probably the case in East Germany as well.

The introduction of democracy and a market economy was generally hailed as a welcome contribution to the quality of life in Eastern Europe. In 1990, the vast majority of the East European respondents polled by the European Commission expressed satisfaction with the development of democracy and with the notion of a market economy. But the picture that emerges from tables 5.3 and 5.4 is not entirely without contradictions. In Poland and Czechoslovakia, only a handful of the respondents (7.6 and 14 per cent respectively) say they are not at all satisfied with the development of democracy. In Bulgaria and Hungary, more than twice as many respondents (24 per cent and 32.5 per cent respectively) adopt an equally critical attitude towards the way democracy is developing. In Poland, Czechoslovakia and Hungary sizeable minorities of almost 20 per cent rule out the market economy as wrong. In Bulgaria, almost 35 per cent of the respondents take this position.

The between-country variations make rather good sense in view of the developments leading up to and surrounding the breakdown of communism of 1989–90 in these four countries. Poland's road from communism to democracy had been marked by political, rather than economic, reforms; and by the late 1980s, Poland already had a long history of dialogue and successful negotiations between government and opposition. Hungary had long had an emphasis on economic reform, and by the time the economic reforms spilled over into political reform, Poland was already well ahead of Hungary (see chapter 4). Czechoslovakia and Bulgaria were latecomers to the political and economic reform processes, but Czechoslovakia moved ahead with the reforms with much more by way of determination once the *ancien régime* had been removed. These circumstances go a long way towards accounting for the between-country differences with respect to the development of democracy. They even render the surprisingly large gap between Poland and Hungary more plausible than it would otherwise have been.

The early evaluations of the emerging market economies of Eastern Europe lend themselves to rather straightforward interpretations. Some 17 per cent to 18 per cent of the respondents in Poland, Czechoslovakia and Hungary reject the market economy as wrong. That is quite a lot but pretty modest compared to Bulgaria, where twice as many or almost 35 per cent of the respondents condemn the market economy as basically wrong. This is roughly what might have been expected considering the elections of Poland, Czechoslovakia, Hungary and Bulgaria in 1989–90. In the three former countries, the electoral wind had favoured conservative coalitions bent on rapid economic reform. In Bulgaria it had propelled a reformed communist party to power on a platform of very careful economic reform. The 1990 Eurobarometer data on the pace of economic reform would seem to support this interpretation (table 5.5). The question was unfortunately not included in the Hungarian questionnaire, but the data from the remaining three countries are rather suggestive. Of the respondents in Czechoslovakia and Poland, 25.2 and 32.4 per cent respectively say they think that the economic reforms are being introduced too fast. In basically socialist Bulgaria, however, less than 2 per cent express this attitude.

One final observation may be in order on the basis of the early Eurobarometer data. With the benefit of hindsight, it is readily apparent that the early election results in Poland, Hungary and Czechoslovakia strongly underestimate the protest potential within the respective political systems. This is perhaps most obvious in Hungary, where sizeable minorities question the development of democracy as well as the potential benefits of a market economy. But it is no less obvious in Poland and Czechoslovakia, where large groups reject capitalism as fundamentally wrong and even larger groups dissociate themselves from the current pace of economic reform. The demise of the victorious right-wing coalitions in Poland, Czechoslovakia and Hungary was not imminent, but the writing was in a sense already on the wall in 1990.

The picture becomes more complex when the time series is expanded from 1990 to 1995, the latest East European Eurobarometer so far. There are fluctuations over time. With a trend towards high or rising levels of discontent with democracy and capitalism which remained stable until 1995, the fluctuations testify to a drawn-out learning experience including early joy and expectations, subsequent disappointment and, most recently, some kind of normalization. The Hungarians have remained strongly critical of the development of democracy throughout the entire time period, though more so at the beginning than at the end. They become much more likely to rule out capitalism as fundamentally wrong as time goes by, but somehow the vast majority of them do not feel that the economic reforms are being implemented too fast. In Poland the level of dissatisfaction with the development of democracy also fluctuates in a way which testifies to the presence of an underlying learning process. The dissatisfaction rate jumps from less than 8 per cent in 1990 to over 20 per cent in 1991 and in 1994, only to drop to the 1990 level in 1995. Similar comments apply to the share of the respondents who rule out the market economy as wrong. It increases by almost ten percentage points between 1990 and 1991 (from 18.4 per cent to 27.1 per cent) and lands at an even higher level (31.5 per cent) towards the end of 1994, only to reach an all-time low of 14.9 per cent in 1995. About one third of the respondents felt that the economic reforms were being implemented too fast at the peak of Tadeusz Masowiecki's austerity programme in 1990–91, but this figure subsequently dropped to slightly more than 18 per cent in 1994. With 14–16 per cent of the respondents expressing dissatisfaction with the development of democracy, Czechoslovakia

Table 5.3 Percentage of respondents not at all satisfied with the development of democracy

Country	1990	1991	1992	1993	1994	1995
Estonia		16.7	25.7	15.6	21.6	14.9
Latvia		12.0	23.8	17.2	24.4	17.5
Lithuania		7.6	5.4	14.7	17.2	19.0
Poland	7.6	20.7	20.3	11.0	20.6	8.5
Czech Rep.	14.0	16.0	11.1	11.5	13.8	10.9
Slovakia	14.0	16.0	17.1	22.0	26.0	18.8
Hungary	32.5	23.1	29.5	31.8	25.9	31.0
Romania		8.3	26.5	15.9	19.8	11.1
Bulgaria	24.0	17.1	24.7	42.3	50.9	34.2
Slovenia			6.5	13.8	16.1	13.1
Macedonia			23.0	23.1	27.3	16.5
Albania		12.2	15.8	12.3	18.2	11.6

*Eurobarometers Nos. 2–6 were carried in mid or late autumn throughout the entire region. Eurobarometer No. 1 was carried out in 1990, but at different points in time, in Poland, Czechoslovakia (which remained a federal republic through 1991), Hungary and Bulgaria.

Source: Eurobarometers East (Nos. 1–6).

stands out as somewhat of a model democracy at the beginning of the 1990s. The Czech Republic – one of the two independent states to emerge out of the so-called velvet divorce – picks up this tradition and lands on a dissatisfaction level hovering around 11 per cent, while Slovakia – the other successor state – may be seen to embark on a path reminiscent of the Polish pattern (from 17.1 per cent in 1991 to 26 per cent in 1994 and back to 18.8 per cent in 1995). The notion of a market economy was never accepted without reservations in the Federal Republic of Czechoslovakia. In 1990, 17.8 per cent of the respondents rejected it as fundamentally wrong; in 1991, 24.7 per cent of the Czechoslovaks condemned the market economy as wrong and, with the dissolution of the federal republic, rejection became even more pronounced and has remained around 40 per cent in the Czech Republic. In Slovakia, rejection increases from a 40 per cent to a 50 per cent level between 1992 and 1993, only to drop back to the 40 per cent level in 1995. The pace of economic reforms was a source of

Table 5.4 Percentage of respondents evaluating the market economy as wrong

Country	1990	1991	1992	1993	1994	1995
Estonia		29.7	37.6	31.9	41.3	34.2
Latvia		30.7	53.3	44.6	51.3	39.6
Lithuania		12.5	21.8	26.8	40.5	28.0
Poland	18.4	27.1	30.4	28.0	31.5	14.9
Czech Rep.	17.8	24.7	37.2	40.9	42.7	36.0
Slovakia	17.8	24.7	42.7	50.0	49.1	39.7
Hungary	16.9	14.9	24.4	35.2	34.7	33.8
Romania		57.7	27.0	31.4	22.5	21.0
Bulgaria	34.6	21.0	26.6	34.4	51.8	33.0
Slovenia			26.1	47.1	37.7	37.5
Macedonia			63.1	61.4	59.3	36.5
Albania		19.5	21.7	22.6	28.0	15.8

* Eurobarometers Nos. 2–6 were carried in mid or late autumn throughout the entire region. Eurobarometer No. 1 was carried out in 1990, but at different points in time, in Poland, Czechoslovakia (which remained a federal republic through 1991), Hungary and Bulgaria.

Source: Eurobarometers East (Nos. 1–6).

concern to one citizen out of four in Czechoslovakia of the early 1990s. By 1994, it inspired 28.7 per cent of the Czechs, but only 14.7 per cent of the Slovaks with fear, which might be attributed to the slightly more dynamic approach to market reform by Václav Klaus as compared to Vladimir Meciar.

In Bulgaria in the early 1990s, the dissatisfaction with the development of democracy went down from 24 per cent to 17.1 per cent, but only to embark on un unbroken upward trend culminating in an all-out dissatisfaction rate of more than 50 per cent in 1994. One year later, Bulgarian dissatisfaction with the development of democracy had diminished dramatically to 34.2 per cent, but it is still the highest in Eastern Europe. The Bulgarian assessment of the market economy follows an almost identical pattern, culminating with a rejection rate of 51.8 per cent in 1994 and dropping to 33 per cent in 1995. But the pace of economic reform was never perceived as a serious problem. There was an increase from a meagre 1.9 per cent in 1990 to 8.1 per

Table 5.5 Percentage of respondents rejecting the pace of economic reform as too fast

Country	1990	1991	1992	1993	1994
Estonia		14.9	11.9	9.3	11.1
Latvia		14.4	18.7	11.9	12.8
Lithuania		22.8	30.7	13.4	16.9
Poland	32.4	33.5	17.1	27.0	18.3
Czech Rep.	25.2	24.5	21.0	19.2	28.7
Slovakia	25.2	24.5	17.8	14.0	14.7
Hungary		15.8	16.1	23.2	16.0
Romania		32.5	23.3	19.5	14.7
Bulgaria	1.9	6.6	14.9	3.7	8.1
Slovenia			8.8	17.3	14.6
Macedonia			8.7	12.6	16.8
Albania		5.0	10.4	20.2	21.0

* Eurobarometers Nos. 2–5 were carried in mid or late autumn throughout the entire region. Eurobarometer No. 1 was carried out in 1990, but at different points in time, in Poland, Czechoslovakia (which remained a federal republic through 1991), Hungary and Bulgaria. This question was not asked in 1995.

Source: Eurobarometers East (Nos. 1–5).

cent in 1994 with an all-time high of 14.9 per cent in 1992, but the fact remains that the Bulgarians have never questioned the pace of the economic reforms to the same extent as most other East Europeans.

In September–October 1991, a good one and half years after the overthrow of the Ceauşescu regime, as few as 8 per cent of the Romanians say they are not at all satisfied with the development of democracy. By November 1994, this figure had more than doubled, but in 1995 had, nevertheless, dropped to 11.1 per cent – the lowest dissatisfaction rate in all of Eastern Europe with the exception of Poland. In 1990, a majority of the Romanians (57.7 per cent) rejected the market economy, but in late 1995 only 21 per cent of the respondents adopt this rather extreme attitude. The pace of the economic reforms clearly also becomes more and more palatable to the Romanians as time goes by. In 1994, only 14.7 per cent of Romanians may be seen to oppose the reforms that were ruled out as too fast by a third of them three years earlier. To the extent that there is discontent with the Iliescu regime, it obviously has little impact on the attitudes of the Romanians towards democracy and market reform.

Albania and the former Yugoslav republics of Slovenia and Macedonia also follow the Polish pattern of increasing dissatisfaction until 1994 and a sudden dramatic drop in 1995. But they do by no means stand out as hotbeds of dissatisfaction with democracy. On the contrary, they start out with basically modest levels of dissatisfaction and end up well within the East European mould. The notion that capitalism is fundamentally wrong increases among Albanians and Slovenes towards 1994 and 1993 respectively, only to plummet to a lower level in 1995. In the Albanian case, the drop in distrust of the market economy is dramatic – the distrust has in fact dropped to an East European low on a par with Poland. Macedonia is a somewhat peculiar case. Between 1992 and 1994 solid majorities in the range of 59 per cent to 63 per cent rejected the market economy as wrong. By 1995, however, the Macedonian dissatisfaction level had dropped to a more normal level of 36.5 per cent. Macedonia displays a similar, albeit less dramatic, pattern with respect to dissatisfaction with democracy. Between 1992 and 1994 the dissatisfaction rate with democracy ranges from 23 per to 27.3 per cent, only to drop as low as 16.5 per cent in 1995. Slovenes and Albanians appear to be stable and strong supporters of democracy. On average, dissatisfaction with the development of democracy in these two countries lies between 7 per cent and 18 per cent throughout the time period.

The three former Soviet republics of Estonia, Latvia and Lithuania are also representative of the overall East European trends. As a rule, there is increasing dissatisfaction with the development of democracy and increasingly negative evaluations of the market economy until 1994 followed by a sharp drop in 1995. The linear trend towards increasing dissatisfaction in Lithuania constitutes the exception, but even so the Lithuanian high of 19 per cent in 1995 is not particularly high compared to the other East European countries.

The Underlying Pattern

The picture may be blurred and confusing at times, but we would nevertheless argue that there is a pattern to the East European response to half a decade of democracy and a market economy. The overall trend is indeed for the East Europeans to adapt to democracy; after rising disenchantment in the early 1990s, few citizens express dissatisfaction with the development of democracy by 1995. There are in fact only three exceptions from this rule, both of them in Central Europe. Hungary – it may be recalled – entered the new age of parliamentary democracy with one out of three questioning the development of democracy. Five years later, this figure had dropped to one out of four which is still high but indisputably less high than at the outset. Similar comments apply to Lithuania. Czechoslovakia – it will also be recalled – was somewhat of a model case with consistently low levels of dissatisfaction at the beginning of the 1990s, a position subsequently defended by the Czech Republic.

The East Europeans are apparently learning to live with a market economy as well; after an initial reform shock in the early 1990s, they were less inclined to reject capitalism by 1995. Again there are only two exceptions from the rule, but this time around the deviant cases are located in the Balkan region. In September-October 1991 almost six out of ten Romanians had reached the conclusion that the market economy was basically wrong; in November 1995 only two out of ten took this rather strong position. In the former Yugoslav republics of Slovenia and Macedonia, scepticism towards the market economy has remained high. Today more than a third of the respondents in those countries reject the market economy. The Slovenian dissatisfaction rate has been stable at this level throughout the time period, but this is not necessarily a sign of economic backwardness. It is in fact the level of dissatisfaction registered in the relatively advanced economies of Hungary and the Czech Republic. With 63.1 per cent in 1992, Macedonia started out with the highest rejection rate ever measured by Eurobarometer East. Between 1992 and 1995, however, the rejection rate dropped to the Slovenian level.

The pace of the economic reforms does not tend to be an increasing source of concern over time, certainly not in Northern Europe or in Bulgaria. But there are four notable deviant cases out of twelve. With more than 28 per cent of the 1994 respondents – as opposed to some 25 per cent in 1990 – rejecting the economic reforms as too fast, the Czech Republic actually comes out at the very top of East European concern about the pace of market reform. The other three countries to display increasing concern about the introduction of market reform – Slovenia, Macedonia and Albania – display considerably more modest levels of concern, but they nevertheless represent a much more profound change of attitudes than the Czech Republic. Bulgaria is a good case in point. An increase of concern about the pace of the economic reform of slightly more than 6 per cent between 1990 and 1994 may not look like very much, but it actually amounts to an increase of more than 300 per cent.

There is a strong element of logic or rationality to the patterns that emerge. There was no doubt a variety of reasons not to be at all satisfied with the development of democracy in Eastern Europe as of 1990 and 1991, but with the benefit of hindsight the vast majority rejected communism as a less attractive alternative than democracy. As memories fade and democracy struggles to establish itself, it becomes more tempting to adopt an all-out critical stance towards the development of democracy, but as democratic procedures are routinized scepticism once again gives way to acceptance.

The democracy item is vague. It does not differentiate between form and content,[9] but there is strong evidence that democracy is evaluated not only from a procedural point of view but also in the light of what it produces or fails to produce. This is clearly the case in Poland, where the economic crisis of the early 1990s results in a substantial loss of confidence in the development of democracy. It is definitely the case in Bulgaria, where even cautious and piecemeal market reforms are accompanied by a rapid decline in the level of satisfaction with the development of democracy. Similar processes are presumably at work in Estonia, Latvia, Lithuania, Slovenia, Macedonia and Albania but *not* in Romania, where a deliberately cautious approach to market reform on the part of the government is accompanied by a remarkable pro-capitalist swing.

Though logical and understandable, the East European response to democracy and capitalism may be a destabilizing factor for the new democracies, but the danger should not be overestimated. The countries of Western Europe also have their fair share of people who are not at all satisfied with the way democracy works (table 5.6). On the whole, the dissatisfaction is not as widespread as it is in Eastern Europe, but this might very well be an artefact of the slightly different wording of the two questions tapping satisfaction with democracy in the two different sets of Eurobarometers.

There is a lot of variation in the West European data matrix which includes countries with extremely low levels of dissatisfaction like Denmark and Luxembourg along with countries like Italy with dissatisfaction rates of a distinctly East European – almost of a Bulgarian – magnitude. An unbroken record of democracy since 1945

Table 5.6 Percentage of West Europeans not at all satisfied with the way democracy works

Country	1991	1992	1993	1994
Belgium	12	14	17	11
Denmark	6	3	3	3
Germany	6	8	11	8
West Germany	5	7	11	6
East Germany	10	12	14	14
Greece	23	20	18	19
Spain	11	17	18	19
France	17	17	15	12
Ireland	16	12	13	7
Italy	33	44	45	25
Luxembourg	1	6	3	2
Netherlands	5	5	6	6
Portugal	4	6	11	10
Great Britain	11	15	14	12
EU (12) average	14	18	19	14

* Eurobarometers have been carried out each spring and autumn since 1973. We have deliberately opted for a time series matching the East European data which have been collected since in mid or late autumn 1991.

Source: Eurobarometers (EB 33,35,37,39).

and a safe distance from the Mediterranean would seem to promote satisfaction with the way democracy works in the West European countries. West Germany fares better on this dimension than the five new *Bundesländer* in the former GDR. Denmark, Luxembourg and the Netherlands do significantly better than Greece and Spain; and Italy – it may be noted – consistently surpasses all the other countries in the table when it comes to dissatisfaction with the way democracy works.

There are obviously factors other than the democratic record and the North–South axis that make themselves felt on the West European data matrix. By way of example, the differences between otherwise similar pairs of countries like Belgium and the Netherlands and Spain and Portugal cannot be accounted for without including a measure of ethnic homogeneity into the analysis. But this is not the main point in this context. The bottomline is that there must be hope for Bulgaria, Macedonia, Hungary, Latvia, the Slovak Republic and all the other

East European countries temporarily marred by widespread discontent with the development of democracy, if Italy, Spain and Greece are already safe for democracy along with the other members of the European Union. Indeed, by 1995, most East European countries had become part of the West European mainstream.

Hope, Yes – But How Much?

If hope there is, the natural question is how much. It would certainly be foolish of us to pretend to have the full answer, but the way respect for human rights changes over time points towards some of the problems facing the new democracies of Central and Eastern Europe (see table 5.7).

Table 5.7 Respondents' evaluation of the governments' respect for human rights: Per cent 'no respect at all'

Country	1991	1992	1993	1994	1995
Estonia	26.1	20.1	11.5	15.3	12.6
Latvia	9.1	16.5	17.1	20.9	14.6
Lithuania	7.6	12.4	30.1	26.8	29.9
Poland	11.6	17.4	16.0	18.5	9.6
Czech Rep.	5.5	5.7	5.6	6.5	7.3
Slovakia	5.5	7.3	12.8	9.7	11.2
Hungary	4.9	9.6	10.8	7.2	10.8
Romania	9.4	17.3	17.3	23.4	13.8
Bulgaria	5.5	10.7	17.8	19.6	13.3
Slovenia		7.0	11.8	13.8	10.6
Macedonia		20.3	19.6	23.9	15.7
Albania	6.0	9.9	10.7	10.9	6.8

* Eurobarometers Nos. 2–6 were carried in mid or late autumn throughout the entire region. Eurobarometer No. 1 was carried out in 1990, but at different points in time, in Poland, Czechoslovakia (which remained a federal republic through 1991), Hungary and Bulgaria.

Source: Eurobarometers East (#2–6).

In September-October 1991 only a fraction of East Europeans took the rather extreme position that the government had no respect at all for human rights. Four years later, in November 1995, the notion that the government has no respect at all for human rights had stabilized at a somewhat higher level (10–15%) throughout almost the entire region. The Baltic states of Estonia and Lithuania are deviant cases with opposite signs. In 1991 Estonians had more serious reservations than the citizens of any other country about the government's willingness and ability to respect human rights; by 1995 the confidence of Estonians in the fairness and even-handedness of the political process had clearly been restored. In 1991, very few Lithuanians (7.6 per cent) – almost on a par with the consistently low Czech level of distrust – felt that the government had no respect at all for human rights, but since then scepticism has quadrupled.

The question about the government's respect for human rights taps at least one central component of what we have previously referred to as the *Rechtstaat*, and it is encouraging that the level of distrust seems to stabilize on the low side in 1995. The turbulence surrounding the human-rights issue in the early 1990s is, nevertheless, understandable in the light of the open ethnic tensions in many of the countries. In Estonia and Latvia, ethnic Russians, many of whom are first or second generation immigrants from other parts of the Soviet empire, found themselves fighting an up-hill political battle against Estonian and Latvian nationalists, who set out to deprive them of political rights they had thus far taken for granted (Dellenbrant 1994a; Crampton and Crampton 1996). Lithuania does not have a Russian-speaking minority of the same magnitude as Estonia and Latvia, but it does have a culturally strong and vocal Polish-speaking minority (Dellenbrant 1994a). Bulgaria was plagued by long-standing strife between the Bulgarian majority and the Bulgarian Turkish minority which had retained a cultural identity of its own since the days of the Ottoman empire; by West European standards, Romania, Slovakia and Albania also had more than their fair share of ethnic tensions and strife.

The increasing disillusionment with the government's respect for human rights in the early 1990s may also be attributed to the confusion still surrounding many of the legal issues that accompanied the transition from communism to democracy and a market economy. We have already referred to the delicate problem of what to do with those officials, managers and leaders who had loyally served the communist state. As of 1990, an overwhelming majority of the East Europeans had been in favour of retaining the services of those former leaders, whose qualifications were real rather than political (see fig 5.1), but not everyone adopted such a conciliatory approach and many East Europeans in countries like Poland, Estonia, Latvia and Lithuania were probably dismayed by the ease with which the old communist *nomenklatura* managed to obtain top-level positions in government and particularly private industry. On top of this, there were the open property and land settlement issues which created a climate of extreme economic insecurity for those occupying contested property or land.

*

These are underlying causes that do not make the disillusionment with the government's respect for human rights any less ominous. But the picture conveyed by table 5.7 is not completely dark. There are in fact a few countries with consistently low levels of disillusionment from 1991 and onwards. These countries – Hungary, the Czech lands and Slovakia – are all located in Central Europe and it is tempting to account for this outcome in terms of the Central European tradition of rule of law. It is not as simple as that, however. The rule of law did not carry much weight under communism and the only countries to edge out of totalitarianism into authoritarianism before 1989-90 were Poland and Hungary, *not* Hungary and Czechoslovakia (see chapter 4). Husak's Czechoslovakia was in fact perceived as a staunch neo-Stalinist regime until it came tumbling down in November 1989 (Bankowicz 1994a).

So, how come the Czechs and the Slovaks consistently trust their respective governments to respect human rights? It does not take much imagination to list a number of factors that may go towards accounting for this outcome. Václav Havel's long-standing record as a dissident and human-rights activists is probably of relevance in this context as is Havel's strong commitment towards rehabilitating the victims and punishing the instruments of Stalinist oppression. But these are country-specific factors.

A closer inspection of the 1994 Eurobarometer data reveals that the attitudes towards the government's respect for human rights are related to age as well as education. In the old Habsburg lands of the Czech Republic, Slovakia and Hungary, it may be noted that the criticism against the government's human-rights record is consistent across age and education, with only a slightly higher level of scepticism among respondents with less than secondary education (Appendix 5.1). As a rule, Poles with higher education tend to be less critical of the government's human-rights record than those with less education, but there is one very significant exception from this rule. Nowhere does dissatisfaction with the government's human-rights performance reach such record highs as among well educated elderly people! Education would seem to exacerbate differences between the age cohorts in Poland. The young tend to be less critical than the old, but the age gap becomes more pronounced with increasing education.

Rough as these indicators might be, they would seem to suggest that people tend to interpret human rights in a rather broad fashion so as to include *not* only freedom of speech, press and public assembly, the protection of property and minority rights frequently referred to in the West but also the socioeconomic rights emphasized by the defunct communist regimes such as the right to employment, to a place to live, to free education and hospital care and to secure old age pensions. It does at any rate make good sense to interpret the outcome of our analyses (see Appendix 5.1) in terms of costs and benefits.

Accompanied as it was by the erosion of the socialist welfare state, the transition to a market economy was painful but probably less so for the young than for the old and less so for the well educated than for those without the benefit of a higher education. In Poland education is decisive; and the age cohorts that take the lead in criticizing the government's human-rights record may be marketed as victims of the transition to a market economy. This certainly applies to age cohorts in the labour market without the benefit of a higher education and to the well-educated Polish senior citizens, who had been hit by one of the most radical austerity programmes in all of Eastern Europe.

Similar comments apply to Bulgaria and Slovenia, where dissatisfaction with the government's human-rights record tends to be more frequent among those without higher education, but *not* to Estonia, Latvia, Lithuania, Albania, Romania and Macedonia, where the impact of education is less strong. Estonia and Latvia, however, display a tendency among respondents with higher education similar to Poland. In all six countries, dissatisfaction with the government's performance on human rights remains widespread among those without higher education, but it is not confined to the less privileged strata to the same extent as it is in Poland. Albania is a case with dubious democratic credentials even today, but the criticism of the government's human-rights record is generally low. This may seem surprising, but less so considering the primitive sultanistic regime that was replaced by democracy – an Albanian government does not need an impressive human-rights record in order to be an improvement over Enver Hoxha and his followers. Even so, the more highly educated tend to be the less critical.

*

It is a moot question how to evaluate all this in terms of prospects for democracy in contemporary Eastern Europe. We have identified three groups of countries. The first group consists of countries where the criticism of the government's human-rights record is very weak but with a slight tendency for the less educated to be more negative. This group consists of the well-developed countries of Hungary, the Czech Republic, Slovakia but also Albania, the least developed country in the entire region. In the second group – Poland, Bulgaria and Slovenia – dissatisfaction with the government's human-rights record seems to be more strongly related to the underlying social stratification. The three Baltic states, Romania and Macedonia comprise a third group where education makes itself less strongly felt. Dissatisfaction with the human-rights record may possibly be dismissed as a problem in the first group of countries. In the second group of countries dissatisfaction with the government's human-rights record may presumably be interpreted as a byproduct of the rough transition to capitalism and is likely to fade out as economic prospects improve. In the third group of countries, dissatisfaction – and for that matter satisfaction – with the government's respect for human rights would seem to boil down to a question of interaction between social class and generation which may prove divisive in the future.

In the final analysis then, the prospects of the new democracies in Eastern Europe would seem to revolve around two factors: the success with which they resolve the transitional problems and the passage of time. This is a conclusion with a certain ring of finality to it, but it must – in all fairness – be admitted that it is of limited predictive value. With Western Europe currently in the doldrums and with substantial economic problems still to be resolved at home, the East Europeans respond to the 1995 Eurobarometer in a way that suggests that Eastern Europe may be on the verge of breaking out of the transitional phase, but the optimism of the young and hopeful may not be taken for granted as they grow older and more experienced. There is certainly hope for the new democracies in Eastern Europe, but it is yet too early to proclaim democracy as the winner in the struggle with dictatorship.

Notes

1. By then, there had already been a number of open confrontations between Soviet military units and the increasingly frustrated Estonians, Latvians and Lithuanians (Dellenbrant 1994a).
2. This was the term generally used in Eastern Europe for socialism in practice as opposed to socialism in theory.
3. Formed as they were to achieve a common goal – independence and/or the defeat of communism – Solidarity, Civic Forum, Public Against Violence and the popular fronts of the Baltic republics were truly heterogeneous political umbrella organizations. This laid them open to internal strife once the common enemy was dead and gone.
4. FIDESZ – the Young Liberals – is sometimes described as the youth movement of the Smallholders, the Hungarian Socialist Workers' Party (HSWP) as a communist successor party and the Social Democratic Party as a party with its roots in the inter-war era (Grzybowski 1994b).
5. In the Baltic republics, the popular fronts had lost their political significance by the first post-independence elections in 1992 (Estonia and Lithuania) and 1993 (Latvia).
6. Transylvania remains an issue of contention between Hungary and Romania; the Košice region in the south-eastern part of Slovakia has by no means lost its explosive potential in the relations between Hungary and Slovakia and the Königsberg–Kaliningrad region in the northern part of East Prussia remains attractive not only to Russia, which annexed this region in the wake of the Second World War, but also to neighbouring Poland and Lithuania.
7. Table 5.1 only pertains to the *Sejm*, i. e. the Lower House, but the Senate – the Upper House introduced in 1989 – was almost equally fragmented prior to the electoral reform of 1993 (Grzybowski 1994a).
8. The East German Institute for Youth Research is a good case in point. It served as East Germany's secret survey research unit, and circulated evidence of increasing dissatisfaction and bitterness among the young about one year before the 1989 October revolution. Somehow this storm warning never reached the top echelons while Honecker remained in charge (*Frankfurter Allgemeine Zeitung*, 25 September 1990).
9. Theoretically this also applies the standard democracy item in the regular Eurobarometer studies, but there does not seem to be much cause to make a case out of it. In 1989 the representative sample of each EU country was split in two so as to remove the impact of partisan considerations from the answers. Fifty per cent of the respondent were confronted with the standard item; the other half were explicitly asked to disregard whether they were for or against the present government, when evaluating the 'way democracy works'. The results of this validity test were disappointing in the sense that there were no significant differences between the two subsamples (*Eurobarometer Trends* 1974–84).

References

Berglund, Sten and Frank Aarebrot (1996), 'Statehood, Secularization, Cooptation: Explaining Democratic Survival in Inter-War Europe – Stein Rokkan's Conceptual Map Revisited', in Stefan Immerfall and Peter Steinbach, Hrsg., *Historisch-vergleichende Makrosoziologie: Stein Rokkan – der Beitrag eines Kosmopoliten aus der Peripherie*, published as Special Issue No. 2, Vol 20, of *Historical Social Research*.

— and Jan Åke Dellenbrant (1994), 'Prospects for the New Democracies in Eastern Europe', in Sten Berglund and Jan Åke Dellenbrant, eds, *The New Democracies in Eastern Europe: Party Systems and Political Cleavages*, 2nd edition, Aldershot, Edward Elgar.

Bankowicz, Marek (1994a), 'Czechoslovakia: From Masaryk to Havel', in Sten Berglund and Jan Åke Dellenbrant, eds, *opus cited*.

— (1994b), 'Bulgaria: The Continuing Revolution', in Sten Berglund and Jan Åke Dellenbrant, eds, *opus cited*.

Bradley, John F. N. (1971), *Czechoslovakia*, Edinburgh, Edinburgh University Press.

— (1992), *Czechoslovakia's Velvet Revolution: A Political Analysis*, Cambridge, Cambridge University Press.

Crampton, Richard and Ben Crampton (1996), *Atlas of Eastern Europe in the 20th Century*, London and New York, Routledge.

Croan, Melvin (1992), 'Germany and Eastern Europe', in Joseph Held, ed., *The Columbia History of Eastern Europe in the Twentieth Century*, New York Columbia University Press.

Dahl, Robert (1992), 'Why All Democratic Countries Have Mixed Economies', in György Szoboszlai, ed., *Flying Blind: Emerging Democracies in East–Central Europe*, Budapest, Hungarian Political Science Association.

Dellenbrant, Jan Åke (1994a), 'The Re-Emergence of Multi-Partyism in the Baltic States', in Sten Berglund and Jan Åke Dellenbrant, eds, *opus cited*.

— (1994b), 'Romania: The Slow Revolution', in Sten Berglund and Jan Åke Dellenbrant, eds, *opus cited*.

East, Roger (1992), *Revolutions in Eastern Europe*, London and New York, Pinter Publishers.

European Commission, *Eurobarometer: Trends* (1974–1994), Luxembourg, Official Publications of the European Communities.

Fischer-Galati, Stephen (1992), 'Eastern Europe in the Twentieth Century: "Old Wine in New Bottles"', in Joseph Held, ed., *The Columbia History of Eastern Europe in the Twentieth Century*, New York and Oxford, Columbia University Press.

Gebethner, Stanisław and Jacek Raciborski (1992), *Wybory '91 a polska scena polityczna'* (Election 91 and the Polish Political Stage), Warszawa.

Gilberg, Trond (1992), 'The Multiple Legacies of History: Romania in the Year 1990', in Joseph Held, ed., *opus cited*.

Grzybowski, Marian (1994a), 'Poland: Towards Overdeveloped Pluralism', in Sten Berglund and Jan Åke Dellenbrant, eds, *opus cited.*

— (1994b), 'The Transition to Competitive Pluralism in Hungary', in Sten Berglund and Jan Åke Dellenbrant, eds, *opus cited.*

Lijphart, Arend (1968), *The Politics of Accommodation: Pluralism and Democracy in the Netherlands*, Berkeley, University of California Press.

— (1977), *Democracy in Plural Societies: A Comparative Exploration*, New Haven, Yale University Press.

— (1991), 'Constitutional Choices for New Democracies', *Journal of Democracy*, Vol. 2, No. 1.

Patáki, Judith (1990), 'New Government Prefers Cautious Changes', *Radio Free Europe (RFE) Report on Eastern Europe*, 13 July 1990.

Reisch, Alfred (1990), 'Historic Vote Brings Democracy Back to Hungary', *RFE Report on Eastern Europe*, 6 April 1990.

Rokkan, Stein, Angus Campbell, Per Torsvik and Henry Valen (1970), *Citizens, Elections and Parties; Approaches to the Comparative Study of the Processes of Development*, Oslo, Universitetsforlaget.

Sartori, Giovanni (1966), 'European Political Parties: The Case of Polarized Pluralism', in Joseph LaPalombara and Myron Weiner, eds, *Political Parties and Political Development*, Princeton, Princeton University Press.

– (1976), *Parties and Party Systems: A Framework for Analysis*, Cambridge, Cambridge University Press.

Tóka, Gábor ed. (1995), *The 1990 Election to the Hungarian National Assembly: Analyses, Documents and Data*, Berlin, Rainer Bohn Verlag.

Wessels, Bernhard and Hans-Dieter Klingemann (1994), 'Democratic Transformation and the Prerequisites of Democratic Opposition in East and Central Europe', Wissenschaftszemtrum Berlins (WZB), Berlin.

Wolchik, Sharon L. (1992), 'Czechoslovakia', in Josph Held, ed, *opus cited.*

Appendix 5.1

In Eurobarometer East No. 5 for 1994, respondents were asked to assess the human-rights record of their governments. In responding, they were given the opportunity to express varying degrees of satisfaction or dissatisfaction with the human-rights record of their respective governments. One response stands out as particularly negative, and at least theoretically detrimental to the notion of democracy and *Rechtstaat*: 'My government has no respect for human rights at all'. In the following diagrams we investigate the effects of generation and education levels on the likelihood of giving this rather extreme response in each of the countries, in terms of the percentage of each age cohort by education level responding 'no respect for human rights at all'.

Figure 5.2 Percentage responding: 'No respect for human rights at all' in Estonia.

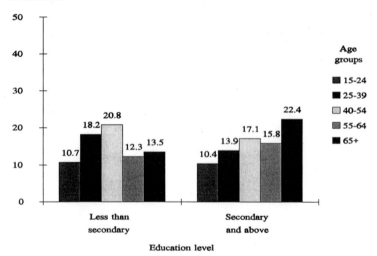

Figure 5.3 Percentage responding: 'No respect for human rights at all' in Latvia.

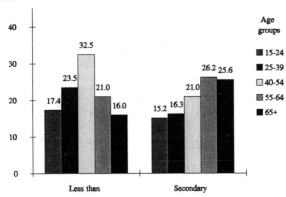

A similar pattern emerges in Estonia and Latvia. Among the better educated there is a clear indication that the likelihood of severely criticizing their government on human rights increases with age. Among respondents with a lower education the occupationally active age cohorts are the most critical.

Figure 5.4 Percentage responding: 'No respect for human rights at all' in Lithuania.

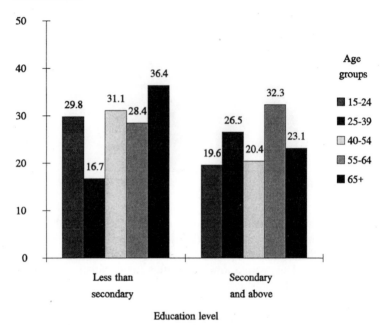

In Lithuania, there is a general tendency for respondents with less education to be more negative towards the human-rights record of the government than the better educated. There is no clear pattern with respect to age.

Figure 5.5 Percentage responding: 'No respect for human rights at all' in Poland.

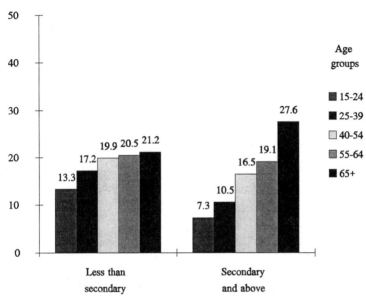

Age is a significant determinant of critical attitudes towards the human-rights record of the Polish government. The older Poles are more negative than the younger. This tendency is clearly most pronounced among the well-educated respondents.

Figure 5.6 Percentage responding: 'No respect for human rights at all' in the Czech Republic.

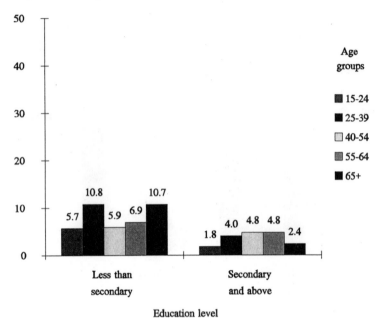

Education level

Figure 5.7 Percentage responding: 'No respect for human rights at all' in Slovakia.

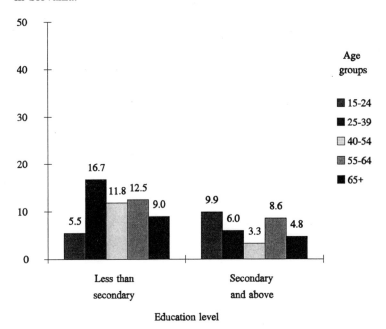

Education level

Figure 5.8 Percentage responding: 'No respect for human rights at all' in Hungary.

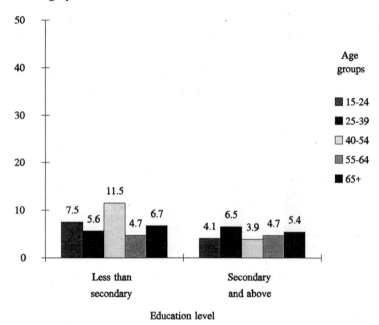

Education level

The Czech, Slovak and Hungarian governments enjoy a low level of severe criticism of their human-rights records. Very few respondents – in all age groups and irrespective of education level – hold the opinion that their governments have no respect for human rights at all. There is a slight tendency for the better educated to be less critical of their governments.

Figure 5.9 Percentage responding: 'No respect for human rights at all' in Romania.

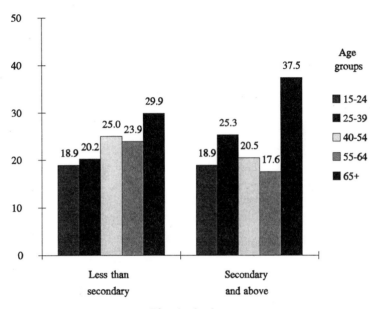

Romanian pensioners, particularly the well educated amongst them, express more negative views about the human-rights record of the Iliescu regime than their fellow countrymen. Generally speaking, the level of criticism is relatively high in all age groups and for respondents with high and low education alike.

Figure 5.10 % responding: 'No respect for human rights at all' in Bulgaria.

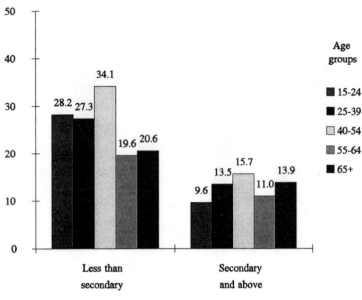

Education level

Bulgarians with less than secondary education are not impressed with the human-rights record of the government, but their better educated countrymen give considerably fewer negative responses. Citizens under 54 years of age with low education form the most negative group.

Figure 5.11 Percentage responding: 'No respect for human rights at all' in Slovenia.

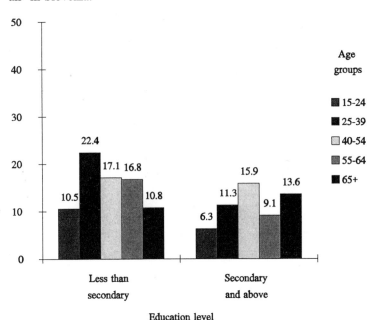

Slovenes in general do not tend to feel that their government has no respect for human rights at all, but respondents with lower education levels tend to be the most negative.

Figure 5.12 Percentage responding: 'No respect for human rights at all' in Macedonia (FYROM).

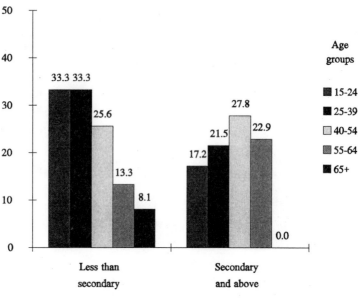

Education level

Pensioners in Macedonia do not condemn their government for human-rights abuses. In fact, not a single well-educated pensioner among the respondents hold the opinion that the Macedonian government has no respect for human rights at all. But people under 54 years of age are among the most critical in all of Eastern Europe, particularly if they do not hold a degree from secondary school.

Figure 5.13 Percentage responding: 'No respect for human rights at all' in Albania.

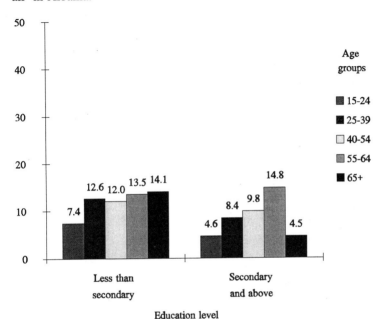

Very few Albanians were of the opinion that their government has no respect for human rights at all. The well-educated are more content than the less educated. Better educated Albanians between 55 and 64 years of age deviate from this pattern. They constitute the most negative group.

6. Prospects and Paradoxes

The Uneven Struggle for Democracy

History has dealt Central and Eastern Europe a democratic option three times in the course of the 20th century: in the inter-war era (1919–39), during the first few years after the Second World War (1945–49) and again in the wake of the velvet revolutions of 1989–90. On the whole, the first two experiments in democracy stand out as failures. The current phase (1990 and onwards) shows much more promise, but the Central and East European region remains marked by its turbulent and conflict-ridden past.

In chapter 1 on the heritage we concluded that the four empires which had dominated Europe all the way through the First World War had been up against three often interrelated challenges – the challenges of nationalism, of territory and of Messianism. These challenges had been instrumental in bringing down the imperial structures, but they did not vanish with the dissolution of the empires – they carried over into the self-proclaimed democratic successor states some of which were miniature Habsburg empires of sorts.

In chapter 2 on the inter-war era we drew the conclusion that the survival or breakdown of democracy was contingent upon three structural determinants: state-building, secularization and cooptation:

> Where the state-building tradition was weak and the legacy of empire strong, or where secular nation-building was still impaired by deeply rooted religious sentiments, or where significant segments representing major cleavages were not coopted into a constitutional compromise, the chances for democratic survival in inter-war Europe were slim indeed (p. 35).

150

This simple and parsimonious model would in fact seem to account for all the democratic breakdown cases as well as for Czechoslovakia, the one and only case of democratic survival in inter-war Central and Eastern Europe. With a complex ethnic structure much like that of the defunct Habsburg empire, an extremely complicated cleavage structure and a highly fragmented party system, Czechoslovakia was in fact a prime candidate for democratic breakdown, saved by intricate consociational devices.

The impact of the three structural determinants of democratic survival is unquestionable. Strictly speaking, however, this finding only pertains to the inter-war era, but the implications are nevertheless manifold. We would expect the countries of Central and Eastern Europe to be more or less capable of coping with the communist challenge with which they were gradually confronted in the wake of the Second World War. The communist claim on hegemony was backed by the overtowering presence of the Soviet Red Army and thus hard to refuse, but it could be accepted immediately and with enthusiasm or only reluctantly and with little or no enthusiasm. We would expect Czechoslovakia, the sole inter-war democratic survivor, and late inter-war democratic failures like and Poland and Germany to be more reluctant than other Central and East European states to settle within the Soviet mould. In a similar vein, we would expect the Central and East European states with an inter-war record of democracy to be more open to pluralism under communism than Russia's other allies.

But, as pointed out in chapter 2, there is also another aspect to it. In the long run, even the most stable macro-sociological relationships are bound to change. The communist parties which were to take over Central and Eastern Europe after the brief semi-democratic interlude of 1945–49 had state-building and socioeconomic change at the very top of the their political agendas; and the primacy of politics, industrialization, urbanization and secularization became the catchwords of the day in the 1950s and 1960s. It would therefore be entirely plausible to draw the somewhat paradoxical conclusion that the prospects for democracy are particularly bright today in those former communist states, where the ruling Marxist–Leninist parties were particularly successful in promoting their pet projects.

Chapter 3 on the democratic or semi-democratic interlude of 1945–49 served to undermine the first set of expectations. With one major exception – Czechoslovakia, which turned left of its own accord and did not need the backing of the Soviet Red Army in order to embrace Soviet-style communism[1] – Central and Eastern Europe would not have turned communist if it had not been for the overpowering presence of the Red Army. The time-table for this process of transformation was not defined by the domestic actors. It was almost exclusively a matter of Soviet national security considerations. In September 1947, Moscow even called upon the Czech and Slovak Marxist–Leninist zealots to speed up the process of transformation so as to keep up the pace with the other socialist countries (see chapter 3).

Domestically defined structural models of explanation are clearly of minor importance in the face of foreign domination. Historically speaking, Eastern Europe is no stranger to subservience to foreign interests. This was, after all, what the old empires had been about. But the Soviet empire that emerged in the wake of the Second World War represented a much stronger call for uniformity than the Ottoman, Russian, Habsburg or German empires had ever dared – or, for that matter, wanted to – raise within their respective spheres of influence. The short Soviet leash was probably necessary in order to make Eastern Europe safe for Stalinism, but in the long run it opened up the entire region for a variety of centrifugal forces. History was free to reassert itself with a vengeance the very minute the Soviet grip on Central and Eastern Europe softened for some reason or other.

This is the theme of chapter 4 on the drawn-out communist parenthesis (1949–89) in Eastern Europe. The chapter focuses on the recurrent crises within the communist bloc – in East Germany as of 1953, in Hungary as of 1956, in Czechoslovakia as of 1968 and in Poland in 1956, 1981 and then again in 1989. These crises were manageable in the sense that they did not have any destabilizing spill-over effects until 1989–90, but in Moscow they were, nevertheless, felt to be serious enough to call for Soviet military intervention or the threat thereof. The grievances and the dynamics of conflict varied from one country to another. In some cases – East Germany 1953 and Poland 1956 – the grievances had distinctly materialistic connotations; in other cases – Hungary 1956, Czechoslovakia 1968 and, for that matter Poland in 1981 – the grievances were cast in a more general democratic rhetoric. In some cases – East Germany in 1953 and Poland in 1956 and 1981 – the protest movement was initiated outside the established political system; in other cases – Hungary 1956 and Czechoslovakia 1968 – the ruling Marxist–Leninist party served as the revolutionary force.

It is worth noting that it was the Central European countries with their historical roots in the Habsburg and German empires, with their inter-war democratic record and with their relatively high standard of living and *not* the Balkan countries with their historical roots in the Ottoman and Russian empires, with their dubious inter-war democratic record and their relatively low standard of living that turned out to be 'accident-prone' as seen from a Soviet vantage point.

The bottomline, however, is that the history of communist Central and Eastern Europe was that of the ruling Marxist–Leninist parties. Theirs was the choice between Soviet-style Marxism–Leninism or careful and guarded reform: and in case of reforms, it was up to the local East European communist party leaders to make the reforms palatable or at least acceptable to their Soviet mentors. Even though a constant hotbed for political dissent, Poland clearly would not have become a champion for pluralism in the mid-1980s, if the ruling Marxist–Leninist party had not been susceptible to dialogue and bent on compromise; and the ruling Hungarian communist party did not have to give up its self-assumed power monopoly, even though it had turned Hungary into an emerging market economy by the mid-1980s.

In theory, there was always yet another option – what became known as the Chinese solution after the dramatic events on Beijing's Tien an Minh Square, when the Chinese political establishment clamped down on the democratic movement in the night of 3–4 June 1989. Moscow had been known to encourage such drastic methods against political opposition within the socialist bloc and the principle of socialist solidarity gave Moscow *carte blanche* to initiate punitive expeditions against allies who failed to suppress the anti-system opposition on their own like Hungary in 1956 and Czechoslovakia in 1968. But, until the introduction of *glasnost* and *perestroika* by Gorbachev, the Soviet Union had little cause to interfere in the internal affairs of the diehard neo–Stalinist regimes of Central and Eastern Europe. The odds were in a sense heavily tilted in favour of an orthodox interpretation of the Marxist–Leninist heritage in Eastern Europe until Moscow's cautious and gradual withdrawal of support from the East European practitioners of Stalinism.

Chapter 5, on the return to pluralism in Eastern Europe in the wake of the upheavals of 1989–90, lends partial, but only partial, support to the somewhat paradoxical conclusion that democracy may have the best prospects today in those former communist countries, where the ruling Marxist-Leninist parties had been particularly successful in promoting socioeconomic change and state-building. It is no easy task to sort out the successful communist regimes from the less successful ones, but some general observations are in order.

The communist call for modernization was universal, but as a rule it was more successful in Northern than in Southern Europe. The communist campaign against organized religion made itself felt throughout the Soviet bloc as well as in Yugoslavia, to say nothing about Albania which proclaimed itself an atheist republic, but it was less than successful in predominantly Catholic countries like Poland and Lithuania. The managerial style of communist Eastern Europe required a powerful state machinery capable of mobilization as well as social control, but the kind of clientelism which had been practised for centuries in Southern Europe does not disappear during a few short decades. The frequent references to the sultanistic features of the Ceauşescu regime in Romania and to the Hoxha regime in Albania and, for that matter, to the feudal heritage of post-communist Bulgaria, testify to the resilience of old patterns of governance.

These observations go a long way towards accounting for the deviant behaviour of Poland in the Central European context, the volatile Balkan response to democracy and market reforms and for the puzzling differences among the Baltic countries, but they are not sufficient to account for the widespread unease about the blessings of democracy and market economy in Eastern Europe. On the whole, however, the chapter ends on an optimistic note. The emerging democracies of Eastern Europe are up against a variety of structural, institutional and attitudinal problems. Some of them – most notably the problem of political fragmentation – are already in the process of being resolved. Others – most notably the dual problems of ethnic diversity and strife – remain largely unresolved. All things considered, however, contemporary Eastern Europe is much better equipped to deal with such challenges than it was in 1919–39, to say nothing about the democratic or semi-democratic interlude of 1945–49 under Soviet guidance. It is in fact highly instructive to approach the current, still ongoing, East European experiment in democracy from a longitudinal comparative perspective.

Figure 6.1 Hegemonies, nationhood and democracy: changing relationships 1900-96

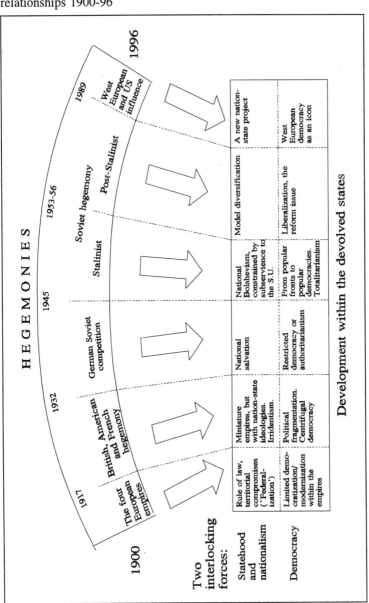

Democracy – The Third Time Around

The semi-democratic interlude of 1945–49 stands out as the most atypical of the three East European experiments in democracy. This time period represents foreign domination and control of such a magnitude that East European politics may be seen as an extension of Soviet national security considerations. The transition of Eastern Europe to totalitarianism by 1948–49 cannot be explained in terms of internally defined structural determinants – nor does it make any sense to do so.

In the latter part of the inter-war era (1933–39), the open competition between Germany and the Soviet Union for a position of hegemony in Eastern Europe threw the entire region into a period of instability and turmoil which served as a prelude to the Second World War (see figure 6.1). Until then, Eastern Europe had enjoyed a period of British, American and French hegemony (1917–32) under the auspices of the principles of the Versailles peace treaties and the League of Nations which favoured parliamentary democracy. It is this early part of the inter-war era that provides the best point of departure for a comparison with the current experiment in democracy that is being carried out in an international climate strongly marked by West European and US interests in promoting democracy in Eastern Europe.

The parallels between the two time periods are obvious, but so are the discrepancies. With all due respect to President Wilson's sweeping references to the importance of making Europe safe for democracy, it is probably fair to say that the British and French architects of the Versailles world order were inspired by a Bismarckian sense for *Realpolitik* at considerable distance from Wilson's idealism. And with all due respect to the East European inter-war leaders, there is very little doubt that they were under the sway of nation-state ideologies which tended to relegate the democracy dimension to a secondary position. In 1989–90 the emphasis in Eastern Europe was on democracy and on cooperation with the West which was seen as the only safeguard against a revival of Soviet imperial ambitions. This West European and Atlantic orientation was not only the gut reaction of recently liberated states, marked by the anti-communist backlash of the early 1990s, but the considered opinion of nations most of which have since experienced government by reform-minded communists as well as by right-wing forces. The East European commitment to the European Community and to NATO is in fact one of the most important factors, perhaps the *single* most important factor, accounting for the continued allegiance to the democratic format in countries with a turbulent and clientilistic past like Albania and Romania.[2]

Indeed, the politics of Central and Eastern Europe in the 20th century is the art of the possible, constrained by two considerations – the type of international regime or hegemony and its consequences for the internal balance between popular involvement in politics on the one hand and territorial consolidation and national salvation on the other. The hegemonies define the rules of the game for the statesmen of Central and Eastern Europe who respond by shifting the balance between democratic considerations and concerns with national safety. Thus, the leaders of the budding political systems of Central and Eastern Europe in what was to become the successor states of the four empires tended to emphasize territorial compromises and national rights while accepting relatively limited suffrage.[3] In figure 6.1 the arrows indicate hegemonic influences on state- and nation-building and democratization in Central and Eastern Europe over time. This chapter focuses on Western hegemony and democratization, but we have previously shown that autocratic hegemonies also provide an impetus for change in Central and Eastern Europe.

*

The ideals of what constitutes nation-states are often constant over time and across regimes, but they may also vary. It is indeed indicative of the fluid and adaptable nature of nationalism that the very definition of nationality may be changed by the political regime in an effort to create new super-nationalities more suitable for the transformation of a multi-ethnic society into a 'national' society. We have already made references to the deliberate attempts to that end by Tsarist Russia in the 19th century (chapter 1). A national state needs a dominant core population and the pan-Slavic ideology was used to provide Russia with such a dominant ethnic group. All Slavic speakers of Russia, with the possible exception of the Poles, were defined as Russians. Thus Ukrainians were referred to as 'little Russians' – a label many Ukrainians gladly adopted. Similarly, the regime often referred to Russians as 'great Russians'. The non-Polish inhabitants of the former Polish-Lithuanian empire were known as 'white Russians' or Belorussians. Among the latter, Tsarist nation-building was so successful that they chose the name of Belorussia for their new independent state after the collapse of the Soviet Union.

In Central and Eastern Europe, however, the self-proclaimed nation-state ideals of varying regimes have in general remained constant over time. In the inter-war era, the definition of nationhood in Estonia and Latvia rested on the twin pillars of majority languages and Lutheranism just as it does today, in spite of the radical changes in the ethnic composition of their respective populations. Similarly, the combination of majority languages and Catholicism has been the nexus of Polish and Lithuanian nationhood, despite enormous territorial changes in the aftermath of the Second World War. In Bulgaria, Orthodoxy and Bulgarian have remained the defining characteristics of the nation-state since the days of the gradual dissolution of the Ottoman empire in the 19th century. The varying regimes of the three remaining non-Slavic nations of the area, Hungary, Romania and Albania, have rested comfortably on a language-based definition of nationhood throughout their modern history. The self-proclaimed definition has been sustained in all the three countries under two conditions: the popular perception of living in a 'sea of Slavs' and the fact that they all have sizeable diaspora populations living in neighbouring countries. Macedonia is a peculiar case which may still be classified as 'stable' in terms of national ideology. Stability across regimes is a meaningless concept in a new state with no modern pre-history. Nevertheless, Macedonia had a strong – even violent – nationalist movement in the inter-war period, and a Macedonian identity was cultivated on a regional level in Tito's Yugoslavia. The relative content of consecutive rebellious, regional and national ideologies is, however, quite stable. It is a strange mixture of different attitudes to different neighbouring ethnic groups which, unlike the Macedonians, had enjoyed statehood for more than a century. The attitude towards Greece is one of inclusiveness, the Macedonians claim a common historical heritage, strongly rejected by the Greeks. The attitudes towards Bulgaria is the perfect mirror image. In this case, it is the Bulgarians who have propagated inclusiveness by periodically claiming that the Macedonians are in reality Bulgarians – a view shared by many Greeks. The Macedonians reject this proposition. In addition to this strange dualism, there is a large Albanian diaspora population in Macedonia and a fear of Albanian irredentism. Furthermore, there is also widespread fear of Serbian imperialism, made more acute by recent events in the Balkans. But this definition of nationhood, almost exclusively related to disagreements with neighbours, has constituted the core of a relatively stable Macedonian national identity. This reactive nationalism has proven its stability at times of rebellion, at times of regional autonomy and today, under independence.

In Poland, Bulgaria, Hungary, Romania and Albania the nation-state ideals were largely unchanged under communist rule. The anti-Semitic campaigns in the People's Republic of Poland and the systematic denial of the existence of a German community in post-war Poland testify to this (Hellén 1996). The Bulgarian communist regime also adopted the traditional nation-state concept. Todor Zhivkov's persecution of the Turkish-speaking minority and the pressures brought to bear on the Bulgarian-speaking Muslims, the Pomaks, are cases in point (Crampton and Crampton 1996). The communist regimes of Romania and Hungary maintained their respective nation-state ideals which were reinforced by the constant conflicts between the two countries over the plight of the Hungarian minority in Transylvania (Hellén 1996). Finally, in Albania open enmity towards Yugoslavia over the Albanian majority in the Kosovo province of Serbia served as one of the pillars of the sultanistic and isolationistic Hoxha regime.

In the above countries the pre-war democracies and autocracies, the communists regimes and the new democracies all seem to share the same basic definition of nationhood. This sets them apart from the two countries which we described as mini-empires, when they emerged as independent states in the wake of the First World War: Czechoslovakia and Yugoslavia. Here, the very definition of nationhood has changed dramatically since communism broke down in the late 1980s and early 1990s. The rulers of Czechoslovakia and Yugoslavia were nation-builders in the sense that they imposed a new definition of nationhood in order to create a strong core population. Old ethnic groups found themselves defined as 'Czechoslovaks' and 'Serbo-Croats' or even as 'Yugoslavs' as seen in some statistics published by the Tito regime. While these definitions included enough linguistic groups to constitute a solid majority, other linguistic groups were excluded and defined as minorities.

With the demise of these mini-empires, a new definition of nationhood was instated. This new definition is very similar to the ideals of the nation-state found in the countries which have retained a constant concept of nationhood across regimes throughout the 20th century. The Czech Republic, Slovakia, Slovenia, Croatia and Macedonia have all opted for a more limited linguistic definition –

albeit in the Slovak and Croatian cases with overtones of Catholicism – as compared to the extensive politico-linguistic considerations of statecraft employed by the defunct mini-empires.

In the case of the Czech and Slovak republics this is clearly visible when we compare the labels of the official statistics of the ethnic composition in the inter-war period with those of the current statistics. In the Czechoslovak censuses of 1921 and 1930, the core group was defined widely as people of 'Czechoslovak' nationality. No more than 65 per cent of the population could be subsumed as belonging to the national core of this 'nation-state'. The minorities, i.e. those citizens who were not considered Czechoslovak, counted Germans, Ruthenians, Magyars, Poles and Jews. The nationalities excluded from the core thus consisted of Slavic as well as non-Slavic speakers, and one excluded group, the Jews, was not linguistically defined at all. The Gypsies were not even listed. The Czechoslovak core population counted Czechs, Moravians and Slovaks. The 1991 censuses list Czechs and Slovaks as the largest groups of the Czech and Slovak republics. Interestingly enough, the Moravians are reported as a minority group in both countries along with diaspora Czechs in Slovakia and Slovaks in the Czech Republic. Germans and Magyars are reported as minorities in both countries, as are Ruthenians in the Slovak census and Poles in the Czech counterpart. Ukrainians appear as a new registered minority in both countries. The remaining Jews are no longer counted as an ethnic minority group, but the Gypsies have been added to the list in the 1991 census in both countries. The definition of the core group is apparently much narrower today, but with more than 80 per cent of the national grand totals these narrowly defined majority groups, nevertheless, account for considerably more than the 65 per cent reported for the Czechoslovak nationality in the censuses of 1921 and 1930.

Similar observations can be made upon comparing the official statistics of Yugoslavia in the inter-war period with current censuses in the successor states. The old Serbo-Croat nationality has been discarded. It goes almost without saying that the Serbs living in Croatia and the Croats remaining in Serbia under present conditions are classified as minorities in the two states – to the extent they dare disclose their nationality to the census taker. Under communism even answering to Yugoslav nationality was possible, albeit not mandatory, for Serb, Croat and Slovene respondents. It should be borne in mind that the very name of this state – the State of the Southern Slavs – came to be regarded as the typical example of proclaimed nationality.

Table 6.1 Ethnicity and proximity to the nation-state model since 1920

Ratings of ethnic homogeneity in terms of the relative size of the regime-proclaimed majority nationality (% of total population)

Country	Majority population	Censuses* 1920	1930	1993
Stable approximate nation-states: Stable definition of the majority nationality, large majorities.				
Lithuania	Lithuanians	81_{1923}		80_{1992}
Hungary	Magyars (Hungarians)			97_{1992}
Bulgaria	Bulgarians	83	87_{1934}	90**
Albania	Albanians			
Newer approximate nation-states: Stable definition of the majority nationality, large majorities today, but smaller majorities in the inter-war period.				
Poland	Poles	70***	70***	99
Romania	Romanians		72	89
Recent approximate nation-states devolved from dissolved 'mini-empires', large or medium large majorities today, small majorities or minorities prior to the recent dissolution of the 'mini-empire' states.				
Czechoslovakia	'Czechoslovaks'	66_{1921}	67	
The Czech Rep.	Czechs			81
Slovakia	Slovaks			86
Yugoslavia	'Serbo-Croats'	74_{1921}	77_{1931}	
Slovenia	Slovenes			99_{1991}
Croatia	Croats			78_{1991}
Former approximate nation-states with a decreased majority population today.				
Estonia	Estonians		86_{1934}	62_{1992}
Latvia	Latvians		77_{1935}	53
Macedonia	Macedonians			65_{1991}

Notes:* The censuses of the inter-war period are generally unreliable in their estimates of the size of ethnic minorities. The figures are, nevertheless, interesting as expressions of perceived size of regime proclaimed core populations.
Notes:** For Bulgaria's current ethnic population our source only indicates that national minorities are in excess of 10%.
Notes:*** The Polish inter-war estimates are highly questionable. Polish nationality was at last partly determined by the ability of the respondent to understand the census-taker when addressed in Polish (Urwin 1980).

Source: Crampton and Crampton 1996.

The original name for the Kingdom of Yugoslavia was The Kingdom of Serbs, Croats and Slovenes. Renaming it Yugoslavia in 1929 was

pan-Slavic statement with almost Russian and Tsarist
s we know today, Serbs, Croats and Slovenes have come
/engeance.

These attempts at creating politically proclaimed super nationalities in Central and Eastern Europe are projects which, with the benefit of hindsight, must be deemed as failures. 'Czechoslovak Man' and 'Yugoslav Man' are extinct species together with 'Soviet Man'. Of the three projects only the Russian attempt at nation-building may have an after-life – but only in the form created by the Tsar, *not* in Stalin's or Brezhnev's versions. But then, the Russian project was allowed to be in operation at least twice as long as its Czechoslovak and Yugoslav counterparts.[4]

As indicated earlier, there exists an opposite problem today in Central and Eastern Europe, notably in Estonia, Latvia and maybe in Macedonia. These are countries with *decreasing* ethnic homogeneity, but with a linguistically defined and thus limited definition of nation-hood which has remained stable across previous regimes. Moreover, the possibilities of increasing the core populations of these countries are hampered by the fact that the new large minorities mainly consist of a diaspora population of a former imperial ruler, or – in the case of Macedonia – of a potentially irredentist Albanian minority.

In addition to more ethnically homogenous countries devolved from former mini-empires and countries with decreasing national homogene-ity, there are two further types of states in terms of nationhood: stable, approximate nation-states where the ethnic homogeneity has been stable and high since the First World War, and newer nation-states where population changes and border revisions in the wake of the Second World War transformed them from mini-empires with weaker core populations into approximate nation-states with stronger core populations. Examples of the former set of countries are Lithuania, Hungary and Bulgaria; examples of the latter type are Poland and Romania. In table 6.1 we have classified the Central and East European countries into these four groups using as a measure of ethnic homogeneity the percentage of the population which has been reported by the different regimes as belonging to the regimes' proclaimed core – or majority – populations. It should be noted that the main purpose of the table is classification of countries. Estimates in terms of percentages have only been included where relatively reliable international sources are available.

The European house that emerged in the aftermath of the breakdown of communist totalitarianism had more rooms in it than the old and familiar cold war European building of states. In this sense the unification of Germany in October 1991 was unique. All the other recent border changes in Central and Eastern Europe have been byproducts *not* of amalgamation but of secession and/or breakdown. Sometimes this process resulted in new, ethnically homogeneous entities – sometimes it did not. The Czech and Slovak republics are clearly more homogeneous than the federal Czechoslovak republic from which they seceded which in its turn had been more homogeneous than Masaryk's inter-war Czechoslovak republic. Due to a continuous and systematic influx of ethnic Russians into the Baltic region, Estonia and Latvia came out of the Soviet Union with much more by way of ethnic diversity than they had ever had before. On the whole, however, contemporary Central and Eastern Europe stands out as distinctly more homogeneous than its inter-war counterpart (tables 6.1 and 6.2). Hungary remains at square one with respect to Trianon. It was ethnically homogeneous until it embarked on a temporarily successful imperialistic mission in the late 1930s, and it was plagued by a diaspora problem which still makes its presence felt in contemporary Hungarian politics. Poland, however, finds itself in a profoundly different position than that foreseen by the treaty of Versailles. In retrospect, we cannot but conclude that Hitler and Stalin did more than most Polish nationalists to promote the idea of an ethnically homogeneous Poland, albeit on territories not originally coveted even by the most ardent Polish nationalists. The gradual disintegration of the multi-ethnic Yugoslav state formation in the early 1990s has given more of a nation-state flavour to the south-eastern corner of Europe. But with the exception of Slovenia, the successor states are mini-Yugoslavias of sorts and currently serve as a constant reminder of the potentially explosive character of multi-ethnic societies. The large scale ethnic cleansing of the eastern parts of Germany and Poland and of the *Sudetenland* in Czechoslovakia in 1945–47 was *not* unleashed in order to make Central Europe safe for democracy, but in the long run this brutal exercise of retribution and Soviet military power may, paradoxically enough, be functional for democracy in the sense that it promoted the nation-state model.

In the final analysis, the states of Central and Eastern Europe have more reason to don the garments of nation-states today than in the early 1920s. In table 6.2 we have used the Eurobarometer East for

Table 6.2 Estimates of the size of the national core populations based on Eurobarometer East No. 6, 1995

Country	Reporting nationality as:	%
Estonia	Estonian	64.1
Latvia	Latvian	60.1
Lithuania	Lithuanian	87.3
Poland	Polish	99.5
Czech Rep.	Czech	93.4
Slovakia	Slovak	87.3
Hungary	Magyar (Hungarian)	95.7
Romania	Romanian	91.8
Bulgaria	Bulgarian	87.2
Slovenia	Slovene	94,2
Macedonia	Macedonian	75.2
Albania	Albanian	98.6

Source: Eurobarometer East No. 6, Autumn 1995.

1995 to make estimates of the current sizes of the core populations as an independent source from the politics of census taking. The core populations may be seen to constitute overwhelming majorities in most of the cases. Three countries, Estonia, Latvia and Macedonia have achieved new national independence with ethnic structures similar to those of Czechoslovakia and Yugoslavia of the inter-war period. Here, the challenge of ethnicity is still at large.

*

It may also be argued that the current experiment in democracy in Eastern Europe benefits from the laboratory provided by the inter-war era. Inspired as they were by the German Weimar constitution, the inter-war East European constitutions had encouraged multi-partyism to the point of making for a high degree of political fragmentation. The post-communist democracies of Eastern Europe have opted for a variety of oligopolistic devices designed to exclude minor political parties from parliamentary representation such as strict thresholds of registration and parliamentary representation as well as proportional representation tempered by distinctly majoritarian features like French-style two-stage elections[5] and the introduction of single member constituencies. Hungary did so prior to the founding elections in March–April of 1990. Poland held on to the Weimar notion of fair representation for a while, and then followed suit like the other East European latecomers to oligopolistic devices. The net result is that political fragmentation has been all but wiped out in Eastern Europe. There is nothing to prevent parties already in parliament from breaking up between elections, but hasty and ill-considered political divorces had a definite price tag attached to them in the form of threshold requirements to be met in the up-coming elections.

The Eastern Europe that emerged out of totalitarian communism in 1989–90 was more developed, more secularized and better educated than ever before, including the inter-war era. With an agricultural sector accounting for 50 per cent of the GDP, Albania – and Albania alone – stands out as distinctly underdeveloped; and yet Albania boasts a fair number of university students (Crampton and Crampton 1996). The macro-indicators for the more mainstream East European countries are much closer to West European standards; and if education were to be used as a measure of social class, it might even be argued that contemporary Eastern Europe represents distinctly middle-class societies (Hellén 1996). The implications of this are manifold, but given our analysis of the breakdown of democracy in the inter-war era we would definitely be inclined to interpret this part of the communist heritage as potentially conducive to democracy.

Yet another difference between the two time periods, perhaps too obvious to be mentioned, has to do with the legacy of communism in contemporary Eastern Europe. There are admittedly many ways of tapping this dimension and survey data provides but one avenue. We have opted for a strictly macro-sociological approach with success of reform communism in post-communist Eastern Europe as the dependent variable and post-war strength and reform orientation of the communist parties as the independent or explanatory variables. By the end of the Second World War, Eastern Europe did not provide much of a platform for organized communism; and we have, therefore, classified the vast majority of the East European communist parties as weak in 1945–49 (figure 6.2). In fact only three countries – Albania, Czechoslovakia and Yugoslavia – are listed as having strong communist parties at that point in time. Communist parties with a commitment to reforms were a rare species in communist Eastern Europe, particularly those with long-standing, uninterrupted records of

Figure 6.2 The legacy of the communist past

Strength of the communist party 1945-9	Weak		Strong	
Reform orientation 1956-89	Reform oriented	Not reform oriented	Reform oriented	Not reform oriented
	Hungary	Romania	All successor states of the former Yugoslavia	The Czech Republic
	Poland	Bulgaria		Slovakia
	(Lithuania)	(Estonia)		Albania
		(Latvia)		

The communist parties of the Baltic republics did not have the option of reform until the advent of *glasnost* and *perestroika* in the late 1980s. The Baltic countries therefore appear within parenthesis. Lithuania has, however, been classified as reform oriented on account of the reform oriented stance of the Brazauskas government

political and/or economic reform ever since the official Soviet proclamation of the possibility of different roads to socialism in 1956. The way we see it, Czechoslovakia does not qualify in spite of the worldwide impact of the Prague Spring in 1968, when communist party leader Alexander Dubček made an attempt to introduce what he referred to as 'socialism with a human face'. Soviet military intervention put an abrupt end to this bold experiment and Dubček's successors did their utmost to turn the clock backwards. We have, therefore, classified Czechoslovakia – and its constituent parts – along with Albania as the only cases with strong post-war communist parties which rejected the reform option when in power. These are the two – nowadays three – post-communist countries that have turned out to be least susceptible to reform communism. In the Czech Republic, the conservative government of Václav Klaus has succeeded in maintaining its grip on power to this very day. Moreover, the leading opposition of the left, the social democratic party, has its ideological and organizational roots in the inter-war era and *not* within the Marxist–Leninist party. The communist successor party is weak and can hardly be described as a reform party – it is the only such party in Central and Eastern Europe that has retained a communist party label. The Slovak citizens' forum, known Public Against Violence, has also defended its positions of power ever since 1989–90, though thoroughly transformed by Vladimir Meciar into a nationalistic party with a conservative economic policy relative to the existing communist state-owned economic structures of Slovakia. Despite the obvious similarities with the economic policies of unreformed communist parties, the party ideology has a distinct flavour of national conservatism with anti-Magyar overtones. Under these circumstances, there is hardly any room for a genuine communist successor party. In the third case – Albania – the anti-communist movement has also held on to power ever since the founding elections of 1991, most recently by resorting to semi-authoritarian practices like violent disruptions of anti-government manifestations and outright election fraud. Contrary to the Czech and Slovak cases, the Albanian successor communist party is the main force of the opposition. But the fact remains that where communism had a popular mandate in the 1940s and failed to deliver reforms in the 1960s and 1970s anti-communist forces and parties are more firmly embedded than elsewhere in Central and Eastern Europe.

It is a moot question whether it is good or bad for democracy that reform communism remains a viable political alternative in Eastern Europe. We would, however, be inclined to say it is good rather than bad. Exclusion of political elites is always conducive to instability of democratic regimes (Wessels and Klingemann 1984); and, other things being equal, circulation of power among competing political elites is preferable to the monopolization of power by one single political force, whether communist or not.

*

The factors listed thus far – the current West European and US interest in promoting democracy in Eastern Europe coupled with a deeply felt desire in Eastern Europe to join the European Union and NATO, the development in Eastern Europe towards the ethnic homogeneity presupposed by the nation-state model, the skilful use of creative electoral engineering to put an end to political fragmentation, the modernization and secularization of Eastern Europe under communism and a historical legacy that favours inclusion and cooptation of the spiritual heirs to Marxism–Leninism – all tilt the balance in favour of a stable democratic development in contemporary Eastern Europe.

6.3 The Challenging Road to Stable Democracy

There are factors pulling in the opposite direction, most notably the uncertain economic prospects throughout Eastern Europe, the strongly clientilistic heritage, particularly in the Balkans, the inclination towards populism and pronounced generational differences in the approach towards democracy, a market economy and market reform (see chapter 5). Most of these factors made themselves felt with at least the same magnitude during the inter-war era. But at least one set of problems is new to contemporary Eastern Europe – the transition to market economy. In figure 6.3 we have plotted the two relevant variables from the 1994 East European Eurobarometer.[6] The outcome is surprising considering the previous analyses (see chapter 5). The trend-line suggests a correlation of -0.21 between the country estimates of a generally negative assessment of the market economy and the view that the market reforms are being carried out too fast. In other words, in countries where people feel that the reforms are moving ahead too rapidly they also tend not to evaluate the market economy as basically wrong. Conversely, in countries where the population adopts a sceptical view of the market economy in general, people also tend to be more tolerant towards stepped-up market reforms. We are thus faced with two sets of paradoxes with respect to the popular assessment of capitalism in Central and Eastern Europe. First, it is paradoxical to imagine a population emerging from the planned economy of a communist state subscribing to the view that while the market economy is not wrong in principle, the necessary economic reforms are moving too fast. Secondly, and equally strange is the sentiment that the reforms are moving at the right speed or even too slowly but that the market economy is wrong in principle. But the main trend lies between these two contradictory positions: between impatient critics of the market in Slovakia, Latvia and Bulgaria and market-oriented people sceptical about economic reform in Poland, Hungary and Slovenia. The obvious explanation is, of course, that these paradoxes are indicators of economic transition in itself. In the three relatively advanced economies of Poland, Hungary and Slovenia limited capitalism had existed already under communism and few people therefore consider capitalism wrong in principle. When faced with the new problems of inequality and social tension, they naturally blame the economic reform programme of the government. Conversely, in the less developed economies of the Baltic states, Slovakia and Bulgaria, where the previous regime had little or no inclination towards capitalist experiment, the market economy itself is still approached with scepticism, while the economic reforms are considered interesting. In our opinion, the paradoxes of the transition period are likely to fade out as the new economies mature.

Figure 6.3 The relationship between attitudes towards a market economy and economic reforms in the Central and East European countries (Eurobarometer East No. 5, 1994)

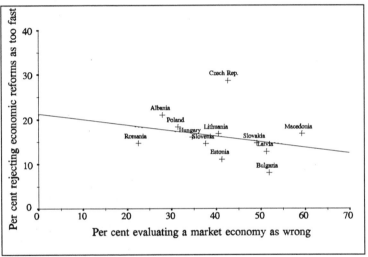

But figure 6.3 serves to confirm the status of four countries – Romania, Albania, the Czech Republic and Macedonia – as clear-cut deviant cases. They are spread over the scattergram and cover it like a rainbow with Romania, the Czech Republic and Macedonia representing the most extreme positions. Romania is notable for its extremely low incidence of ruling out the market economy as wrong; the Czech Republic deserves attention for the extremely large proportion of respondents rejecting the market reforms as too fast and Macedonia for the overwhelming condemnation of the market economy as wrong. The difference between Romania and the Czech Republic is that between a post-communist country constantly under the sway of reform communism and a post-communist country dominated by a right-wing coalition from the breakthrough of democracy in 1989–90 until the present. In Romania the cautious market reforms of the communist-dominated Iliescu regime have resulted in a gradual popular conversion to capitalism coupled with a moderate rejection rate of the pace of the economic reforms. In the Czech Republic the quick and rough transition to capitalism has resulted in a reservoir of built-up discontent with capitalism as such and the pace of economic reforms that may conceivably threaten Václav Klaus and his Civic Democratic Party in the near future.[7] The Albanians are basically favourably disposed towards a market economy but have a strong tendency to condemn the economic reforms as too fast. This sets them apart from the Macedonians, who come out as overwhelmingly critical of the market economy, but only as moderately negative towards the pace of the economic reforms. The difference between these two countries is that between poor post-communist countries under the sway of different political and economic experiences in the immediate aftermath of the demise of Soviet-style communism. It is an open question whether Albanians and Macedonians know what market economy is, but unlike Macedonia, Albania had gone through an election in 1991 where the ruling reform communists were successfully contested by a non-socialist party in an openly ideological election campaign. This conservative coalition was returned to power in the May elections of 1996 which were marked by severe irregularities.

The remaining eight mainstream countries cluster towards the middle of the scattergram and break down into sub-clusters that make paramount sense given our previous analysis. It would in any event seem reasonable to expect to find Poland, Hungary and Slovenia in one group and Estonia, Latvia, Lithuania, Slovakia and Bulgaria in another group. The bottomline is that voters' assessment is contingent upon at least three factors: the relative economic development of their respective countries, their experiences under communism and the policies of the various post-communist regimes. The last factor is not the least important. It is normal in all democracies, not only in those of Central and Eastern Europe, for economic reform programmes to be evaluated by the current content of the voter's pocketbook rather than by his/her perception of history.

History does, however, matter when it comes to the voter's assessment of the development of democracy. As we have demonstrated in chapter 5, the general trend in Central and Eastern Europe since 1990 has been one of normalization. The assessment of the way democracy works has fluctuated over time as a function of the turbulent developments in many of the East European countries. The general trend as of the late autumn of 1995 is towards decreasing dissatisfaction with the way democracy works in Eastern Europe. We would in fact argue that the process of normalization has gone so far as to place the East European regimes on par with the EU countries. In figure 6.4 we have compared the percentage of voters in Central and Eastern Europe as of 1995, who say they are not at all satisfied with the development of democracy in their respective countries, with the percentage of respondents in the EU countries as of 1994, who say they are not at all satisfied with the way democracy works. The wording of the question differs somewhat from one set of Eurobarometers to the other, but we are, nevertheless, confident that the two items tap the same underlying dimension – the assessment of the way democracy works.

A general observation is that dissatisfaction with democracy seems to follow a North–South axis more than an East–West axis. Of the seven countries with the lowest dissatisfaction rates only one – Portugal – is located in Southern Europe; and of the seven countries with the highest only one – Lithuania – is situated in Northern Europe. The two countries with the highest dissatisfaction rates – Hungary and Bulgaria – are indeed East European, but as shown in chapter 5 the Bulgarian dissatisfaction rate has dropped dramatically since 1994. The Hungarian dissatisfaction rate has been stable around 30 per cent ever since 1990. As we see it, this must be attributed to the high level of economic and democratic development during the last stages of Hungarian communism which gave rise to a spiral of higher and higher expectations. The third highest rate can be found in Italy, where a quarter of the population expresses dissatisfaction with the way democracy works. Students of Italian politics would hardly be surprised considering the frequent political scandals and the recent breakdown of the Italian party system. Furthermore, there is a group of countries with dissatisfaction rates in the range of 12 per cent to 18 per cent including not only the Baltic states, Slovakia and the remaining Balkan countries, but also two of the three EU countries – Greece and Spain – which emerged as democracies in the 1970s. The voters of the dominant EU countries – Germany, France and Britain – express dissatisfaction rates in the range of 8 per cent to 12 per cent. Two additional EU countries – Portugal and Belgium – and three East European countries – Poland, Romania and the Czech Republic – also

Figure 6.4 Percentage of respondents very dissatisfied with democracy in own country. The Central and East European countries appear in italics

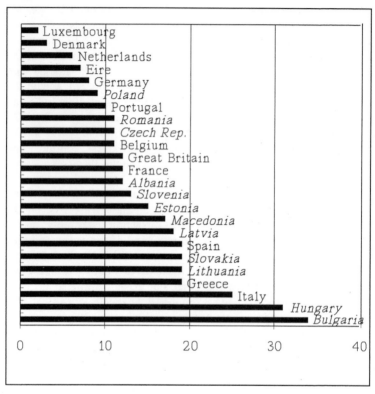

Source: EB East No. 6, 1995 and EB No. 39, 1994.

fall within this range. The countries with the lowest dissatisfaction ratings are all small EU countries in Northern Europe – Luxembourg, Denmark, the Netherlands and Eire.

But democracy can hardly be evaluated only as a concept; democracy is not only an ideal – it is also a way of resolving conflicts. The institutionalization of dissent into a common set of rules for conflict resolution is one of the major challenges facing new democracies. What are the major cleavages in Central and Eastern Europe of the 1990s?

First of all, there seems to be a strong left–right cleavage present in all countries without exception. This is quite natural considering that democracy has developed with a heritage of strong state apparatuses from the previous communist regimes, while the need for market reforms has been at the very top of the political agenda. It is therefore obvious that conflict will arise over how to balance state involvement and the market economy. In fact, an overwhelming majority of the countries have experienced orderly democratic governmental changes as a result of elections fought along a distinct left–right cleavage.

Secondly, the major political formations in Eastern Europe – whether conservative, liberal, social democratic or socialist – share a distinctly secular flavour. This has paved the way for a variety of parties catering to the religious heritage. Christian Social and Christian democratic parties have been organized throughout the region.

Thirdly, the Western ideological predominance and the general commitment to the policies of NATO, the European Union and the World Bank have given the established political parties a cosmopolitan flavour. In a setting strongly marked by nationalism, this has a created a market for nationalistic dissent throughout Eastern Europe. Though basically cosmopolitan, the established parties have been known to exploit such sentiments, but they have also provided a niche for outright right-wing and reactionary nationalistic parties.

In a mature democracy, these three cleavages – left–right, religion and nationalism – should be contained within the democratic polity in the sense that the actors adhere to the constitutional rules of the game. The big question preoccupying students of Central and Eastern Europe today is whether – and to what extent – the new democracies of Eastern Europe meet these requirements and are likely to meet them in the near future. Contrary to the left–right cleavage which is structurally determined, the nationalistic and religious cleavages have historical roots. Understanding these roots is the key to understanding the challenges to the democratic ideals in Central and Eastern Europe.

When discussing the failure of democracy in Central and Eastern Europe in chapter 2, we underlined the importance of the difference between countries, where organized religion was subjected to a dominant state, and countries, where medieval dualism between governmental and religious authority still existed in some form or another. Under communism, dualistic religious authority was eroded, but it is, nevertheless, still present in a number of the East European countries. We have made a distinction between countries with a dominant secularized state and states with remaining elements of religious autonomy: the former group of states includes the Protestant countries and the secularized Catholic countries where the church has a somewhat distant relationship to the Vatican as well as secularized Orthodox countries, where the national religious hierarchy has been the obedient servant of the state for centuries; the latter group counts countries with ecclesiastically oriented Catholic churches, countries with Orthodox churches with some independence towards secular authority and the Muslim countries. It should be noted that all the Orthodox churches of Eastern Europe were the obedient instruments of the communist states. After communism, however, some of these churches have cultivated relations with oppositional religious groups. In the Muslim countries, the rebirth of fundamentalism has strengthened this dualism, albeit to a lesser extent in the European Muslim countries than in the Middle East.

The nationalist cleavage is equally dependent on historical conditions. Today the Central and East European countries range from approximate nation-states to states which still contain strong elements of imperial rule with sizeable and diverse minority groups. There are two types of approximate nation-states in Central and Eastern Europe: states where the dominant national groups almost exclusively reside within the state borders and states with a similarly dominant national group but with people from the same ethnic group living in diaspora in neighbouring countries. There is another set of states which nearly live up the nation-state ideal but which contain vocal and organized diaspora groups from neighbouring countries. The countries, most distant from the nation-state ideal, are identical with the set of countries involved in the dissolution of the Eastern historical empires. Some of them devolved from these empires with a clear nation-state ideology but with sizeable diaspora groups of their former imperial masters. The former empires – Russia and Turkey – also claim to be nation-states today, but with sizeable minorities of other ethnic groups they are contradicted by their own imperial heritage. To make matters worse, some of these minorities have recently expressed demands for autonomy and even sovereignty, inspired by the fact that other former minority groups have succeeded in seceding from the empires. The most notables examples are, of course, the Chechens and the Ossetians of the Russian federation, whose recent national mobilization is inspired by the independence of the former Caucasian republics of Armenia, Azerbaijan and Georgia. Similarly the national mobilization

Figure 6.5 Classification of countries by ethnic diversity, diaspora minorities and religious dualism

| | Reborn and new states with majoritarian national core populations: | | | Reborn states with majoritarian national core populations, but with national minorities comprising the core populations of neighbouring former historical empires | Former historical empires, presently large states with a majoritarian national core population |
| | Approximate nation-states with *dominant* national core populations | | States with strong national core populations, but with active interface minorities from neighbouring countries' core nationalities | | |
	without substantial diasporas in neighbouring countries	with diaspora in neighbouring countries			
Dominant state: Protestant or secularized religious community (National Catholic or secularized Orthodox)	Czech Rep. Slovenia	Hungary	Slovakia	Estonia Latvia Moldavia	Russia The Ukraine Belorussia
States with remaining elements of religious autonomy, dualism: Ecclesiastical Catholic, National or Ecclesiastical Orthodox and Muslim	Lithuania Poland	Croatia Albania	Macedonia Bosnia Romania Serbia	Bulgaria	Turkey

of the Kurds in Turkey has been enhanced by the new autonomous status of their brethren in Northern Iraq.

In figure 6.5 we have juxtaposed the structural conditions of religious dualism on the one hand and deviations from the nation-state model on the other. The Central and East European countries fall into the ten different categories of the table. First of all, the Czech Republic, Slovenia and Hungary must be considered dominant secular states today with an ethnic composition which comes extremely close to the nation-state model. Hungary differs from the other two in that sizeable Magyar minorities live in other countries. Four states – Lithuania, Poland, Croatia and Albania – also come very close to the nation-state model, but they have societies that are less secularized and religious elites therefore have potential for independent action vis-à-vis the state authorities. In addition, Croatia and Albania have diaspora minorities in neighbouring countries. The next group of states – Slovakia, Macedonia and, for that matter, Bosnia – have majoritarian core populations and claim allegiance to nation-state ideologies, but these countries also have vocal and organized interface minorities with the same ethnic background as the core populations of the neighbouring countries. Slovakia differs from the other two in the sense that it is relatively secularized. Romania is a special case. The Romanians clearly constitute the dominant ethnic group and the authorities lean exclusively on this group in terms of political legitimacy. But in addition, Romania has a Magyar minority in Transylvania and in the Banat and a diaspora population which constitutes a majority in the neighbouring former Soviet republic of Moldavia. Estonia, Latvia, Moldavia and – to some extent Bulgaria – form yet another group of states, where the nation-state ideology proclaimed by the core population is challenged by diaspora minorities of neighbouring countries. In Estonia, Latvia and Moldavia, the minority problem is exacerbated by the fact that this is not just any minority, but a Russian minority. The problem is somewhat alleviated by a high level of secularization among the core population as well as the Russians. Bulgaria is a somewhat different case. Its Turkish minority is considerably smaller than the Russian minorities of the three other countries and Turkey is a less awesome neighbour than Russia. Moreover, Bulgaria's devolution from Turkey took place more than a century ago. In this sense, the potential for national conflict is less pronounced in Bulgaria, but the fact that most Turks (and some Bulgarians) are Muslims increases the conflict potential particularly if national minority and religious minority demands are combined. The Russian federation is developing along the lines of a large nation-state in the making. National and patriotic symbols are used intensively to mobilize Russian voters by the democratic forces as well as by the communists. This process of mobilization does not facilitate the integration of the remaining national minorities; nor does it reduce the fears of the neighbouring countries with Russian diaspora populations. Turkey has faced the same problems ever since Atatürk's reforms of 1912. But if Russia were to look to Turkey for solutions, particularly in order to find out if economic growth and modernization can reduce ethnic tension, she would be sadly disappointed. In secularized and modernized Turkey national conflict in the form of the Kurdish rebellion and dualistic challenges in the form of Muslim fundamentalism have come back with a vengeance. Two secularized countries – the Ukraine and Belorussia – are ambiguous cases. Formally speaking, they belong to the same class as Estonia, Latvia and Moldavia, since they are independent states with large Russian diaspora minorities. But in terms of political culture, Ukrainians and Belorussians have been part of the Slavic national core of the Tsarist empire as well as the Soviet Union and in that sense they are similar to Russia.

The placement of the countries in figure 6.5 does not imply that nationalistic and/or religious fervour are absent in some countries and present in others. It does suggest that the resonance and susceptibility for such messages varies with the placement of the countries. If a member of the Czech ultra-nationalistic Republican Party seeks to mobilize Czech voters by invoking the spectre of a hypothetical *Sudeten*-German revival, this is not as detrimental as an Estonian nationalist lashing out against the Russians. In a similar vein, anti-religious, secular agitation is less potentially explosive in the Czech Republic than it is in Poland and Lithuania.

Our basic concern is to demonstrate that the new democracies in Central and Eastern Europe face challenges both to their statehood – ultimately even their territorial integrity – and their nationhood. These challenges vary in severity to the extent that the countries deviate from the dominant secular state model and/or from the nation-state model. This is illustrated by figure 6.6.

The success of democracy is contingent upon its ability to contain challenges as manifest cleavages within the political system. The experiences from the inter-war period clearly indicate that the

5.6 Political cleavages and democratic challenges

Column headings (left to right):

Reborn and new states with majoritarian national core populations:

	Approximate nation-states with dominant national core populations		States with strong national core populations, but with active interface minorities from neighbouring countries' core nationalities	Reborn states with majoritarian national core populations, but with national minorities comprising the core populations of neighbouring former historical empires	Former historical empires, presently large states with a majoritarian national core population
	without substantial diasporas in neighbouring countries	with diaspora in neighbouring countries			

Row headings (top to bottom on left):

Strong states confronted with market reforms have created strong left–right cleavages in all countries

The patterns of further conflicts and cleavages

Dominant state:
Protestant or secularized religious community (National Catholic or secularized Orthodox)

States with remaining elements of religious autonomy, dualism:
Ecclesiastical Catholic, National or Ecclesiastical Orthodox and Muslim

Arrows / diagonal labels:

Challenges to statehood: Territorial integrity

Challenges to the nation-state: The imperial heritage

Challenges to nationhood:
Secular dominance

Cell contents:

Weak: High likelihood of containing challenges as manifest cleavages within a democratic polity

Strong: Possible difficulties in containing nationalism combined with religious or secular cleavages

Strong: Possible difficulties in containing nationalist demands based on separatism or irredentism

Very strong in a situation of a possible combined territorial and religious challenge

cooptation of all conflicting forces was crucial to the survival of democracy at that point in time. When comparing the inter-war era with the present experiment in democracy, we concluded on an optimistic note. The above account of the many structural differences among the Central and East European countries does not give us cause to renege on our optimism as to the prospects for stable democracy in this region. It does, however, suggest that there are countries more in need of careful and intelligent statecraft than others. The seriousness of the need for wisdom is underlined by the fact that all the countries which have experienced or are experiencing civil wars – Russia, Turkey, Bosnia and Moldavia – can be found at the right and towards the bottom of our diagrams 6.5 and 6.6.

What will such statecraft imply? An obvious answer is, of course, to actively discourage extreme rhetoric and political polarization and to institute strong offices of national unity and other consociational devices; both policies were pursued with great success by Finland in the aftermath of the Second World War and, for that matter, during the cold war. Another strategy may be gauged from Robert Dahl's (1966) seminal work on the structuring of cleavages in Western democracies. Dahl's central point is that the challenge to national cohesion is considerably greater if the various cleavages coincide. In other words, given our three dominant cleavages – left–right, religious-secular and nationalist-cosmopolitan – the worst-case scenario would be for all of them to coincide. An example from Western Europe may serve to highlight this problem: the practice of Protestant trade unionists in Northern Ireland to deny Catholics apprenticeships has deepened the sectarian conflict in that society. The task for Estonian democrats today is, therefore, to avoid discriminating residents on the basis of Russian language and religious Orthodoxy. Yet another strategy implies the kind of creative electoral engineering recommended by Sartori (1966; 1976) in order to combat political fragmentation, political extremism and political immobilism. But as we have seen, the advantages of oligopolistic devices are already fully appreciated by the East European political elites.

*

In discussing the impact of communism for the prospect for democratic survival in Central and Eastern Europe today, we reached two paradoxical conclusions. First, the existence of a substantial and stabilizing middle class was found to be contingent upon a modern educational system, created by the communists and capable of producing such a middle class. Secondly, the creation of a strong secular state – one of the pet projects of the communist – is also a *sine qua non* for sustaining democracy in Eastern Europe. Summing up our arguments about the present challenges of dualism and nationalism, we arrive at a third paradox: the greater the electoral potential for mobilization along religious and nationalistic lines, the greater the need to combat and counteract such mobilization.

Notes

1. There is nothing sinister about post-war Czechoslovakia. France, Italy and a number of West European countries also turned left in the wake of the Second World War, but unlike Czechoslovakia, they were not located within the Soviet sphere of influence with all the opportunities which that opened up for the communists.

2. The partial rerun of the June 1996 elections in Albania – which were criticized by the electoral observers for widespread irregularities – testifies to the importance of the Western connection. Similar comments apply to the gradual improvement of the Romanian electoral record.

3. This choice of nationalist mobilization within new state borders at the expense of general democratic mobilization is not self-evident. The opposite priority – that of combining national and democratic mobilization without questioning the territorial integrity of the empire – was the main strategy of revolutionaries in 1848 throughout Central and Eastern Europe. With Hungary as the only possible exception, this strategy turned out to be an abysmal failure which may go towards accounting for the strategic priorities of 1918.

4. We date the Russian nation-building project back to the attempts to establish a pan-Slavic empire in the 1860s as part of the Tsarist reform programme (Tilly 1993).

5. Since 1958 French elections are a two-stage affair, where the first round serves to define who will participate in the final and decisive round.

6. The item about the pace of economic reforms was not included in the 1995 Eurobarometer.

7. This all but materialized in the May elections of 1996 which spelled success for the social democratic party – the only East European social democratic party with roots almost exclusively in the inter-war era rather than within Marxism–Leninism.

References

Crampton, Richard and Ben Crampton (1996), *Atlas of Eastern Europe in the 20th Century*, London and New York, Routledge.

Dahl, Robert A. (1966), *Political Oppositions in Western Democracies*, New Haven, Yale University Press.

Hellén, Tomas (1996), *Shaking Hands with the Past: Origins of the Political Right in Central Europe*, Helsinki, The Finnish Society of Sciences and Letters and the Finnish Academy of Science and Letters.

Sartori, Giovanni (1966), 'European Political Parties: The Case of Polarized Pluralism', in Joseph LaPalombara and Myron Weiner, eds, *Political Parties and Political Development*, Princeton, Princeton University Press.

— (1976), *Parties and Party Systems: A Framework for Analysis*, Cambridge, Cambridge University Press.

Tilly, Charles (1993), *Die Europäischen Revolutionen*, München, C. H. Beck Verlag.

Urwin, Derek (1980), *From Ploughshare to Ballot Box: The Politics of Agrarian Defence in Europe*, Oslo, Universitetsforlaget.

Wessels, Bernhard and Hans-Dieter Klingemann (1994), 'Democratic Transformation and the Prerequisites of Democratic Opposition in East and Central Europe', Wissenschaftszentrum Berlins (WZB), Berlin.

Index of Names

183

Index of Subjects